Key Financial
Instruments

Endorsements

A macro approach to understanding derivatives. Edwardes not only understands the mechanics of derivatives, but more importantly, has a deep understanding for the big picture. Read it, then read it again. *Fred Balcom, Senior Account Manager, FinancialCAD Corporation, Vancouver*

If you haven't attended a Warren Edwardes speech, or lecture, this book is the next best thing. If you have, then you'll want to relive it through these pages. I found it very well written. Professionally superb work. *Professor S. J. Chang, Professor of Finance, Illinois State University, Illinois*

For those who wish to discover the delightful world of derivatives without the daunting task of understanding the usual gobbledegook, *Key Financial Instruments* is the decisive, dazzling read of the decade. *Jim Courtney, Publisher, Global Trading, London*

A comprehensive and thorough coverage of the finer points of derivatives and financial engineering. Edwardes' clear and succinct explanations show how financial engineering can be used to reduce uncertainty and improve returns in an uncomplicated manner. *Peter Feltis, Senior Manager, Corporate Advisory, Banque Nationale de Paris, Seoul*

This book certainly lives up to the title. In plain English he provides a thorough understanding of derivatives, in terms of the instruments themselves and aspects of the instruments (e.g. risk, tax and legal aspects). A useful tool for all managers involved with derivatives that also functions effectively as a reference. *Julian Fry, Assistant Vice-President, European Derivatives, Merrill Lynch Europe, London*

A refreshing demystifying book on derivatives from someone who has leading-edge experience and the ability to communicate clearly in an engaging style. *Professor Alan Grimshaw, Chairman, Department of Finance, Towson University, Maryland*

In his original and colourful way, Professor Warren Edwardes simplified the subject of derivatives to me during his lectures in Korea. Those who find derivatives complicated will share my enlightenment on reading his book. *Chung-Woo Kim, Manager, International Finance Department, Korea Development Bank, Seoul*

Warren Edwardes' first book has been well worth waiting for. It provides valuable insights from someone with over two decades of derivatives experience as a developer, end-user, adviser and a trainer. *Dr Edmond Levy, Assistant Director, Specialized Derivatives Group, HSBC MIDLAND, London*

There are innumerable books on finance that tell you 'how?'. This book aids understanding by explaining 'why?'. *Dr Stefania Perrucci, Consultant, Finance Policy Department, IFC, World Bank Group, Washington*

Edwardes' considerable practical experience is evident in this book. His ability to communicate the intricacies of derivatives makes it is easy to read and even easier to understand. *Carlos Serrano, Deputy Manager, Global Financial Institutions Group, Investment Banking Division, Banco Bilbao Vizcaya, Madrid*

In the expanding world of derivatives a down-to-earth guide is always helpful. Warren Edwardes' book covers a wide range of topics in this area and will be a useful resource. *Julian Walmsley, Managing Director of Askeaton Associates Ltd., London; Visiting Research Fellow, ISMA Centre, University of Reading, author of 'Guide to Foreign Exchange and Money Markets'.*

Professor Edwardes' book brings derivatives to life. This book is the ultimate 'user manual' for DIY enthusiasts and finance market cognoscenti. Derivatives are a useful tool in the hands of the informed practitioner but the uninitiated or overtly reckless should not be let loose on them. *Anne-Maria Wilfling-Rothenstein, European Head of Sales, Treasury & Capital Markets, KBC Bank, Brussels*

FINANCIAL TIMES
Prentice Hall

In an increasingly competitive world, it is quality of thinking
that gives an edge. An idea that opens new doors, a
technique that solves a problem, or an insight that simply
helps make sense of it all.

We work with leading authors in the fields of management
and finance to bring cutting-edge thinking and best
learning practice to a global market.

Under a range of leading imprints, including *Financial
Times Prentice Hall,* we create world-class print publications
and electronic products giving readers knowledge and
understanding which can then be applied, whether studying
or at work.

To find out more about our business and professional
products, you can visit us at **www.businessminds.com**

For other Pearson Education publications, visit
www.pearsoned-ema.com

Key Financial Instruments

Understanding and innovating in the world of derivatives

Warren Edwardes

Jenine.

All the best & Thanks for all the help.

Warren

FINANCIAL TIMES
Prentice Hall

An imprint of **Pearson Education**

London · New York · San Francisco · Toronto · Sydney
Tokyo · Singapore · Hong Kong · Cape Town · Madrid
Paris · Milan · Munich · Amsterdam

PEARSON EDUCATION LIMITED

Head Office:
Edinburgh Gate
Harlow CM20 2JE
Tel: +44 (0)1279 623623
Fax: +44 (0)1279 431059

London Office:
128 Long Acre
London WC2E 9AN
Tel: +44 (0)20 7447 2000
Fax: +44 (0)20 7240 5771
Website: www.business-minds.com

First published in Great Britain 2000
© Pearson Education Limited 2000

ISBN 0 273 63300 7

British Library Cataloguing in Publication Data
A CIP catalogue record for this book is available from the British Library.

10 9 8 7 6 5 4 3 2 1

Typeset by M Rules
Printed and bound in Great Britain by Biddles Ltd, Guildford & Surrey

The publishers' policy is to use paper manufactured from sustainable forests.

Dedication

This book is dedicated first and foremost to Esperanza, my wife, for her patience, support and encouragement.

I thank my colleagues, clients and students who have encouraged me to write such a book over the years. I particularly thank Alan McRae for commenting on parts of the manuscript. Of course, I take full responsibility for the contents, except for the chapter on legal risks written by Iona Levine, whom I thank. Iona Levine is partner and head of the Derivatives practice at Hammond Suddards, and author of *Derivatives: Law & Documentation*, published by Sweet & Maxwell. Farrukh Imran Younus assisted with the appendix on Islamic Banking.

Of course, this book would not have been written were it not for the invitation of the publishers, Richard Stagg and Amelia Lakin, and I thank them for their patience.

Finally, thanks are due to Ralph and Emilio. Ralph is my father-in-law's Alsatian dog. He kept me company on my inspirational walks in *Can Pelegrì* in Serinyà in Girona, Spain. This is a book about innovation in financial markets. Amongst other businesses, the internet and communication technology is radically transforming financial markets and publishing. *Key Financial Instruments* was commissioned by the London publishers in the age of the internet when I was in Korea, and submitted to them via e-mail, using a mobile phone attached to a sub-notebook computer in a farm in the Pyrenees foothills in Northern Spain. 'Emilio' is Spanish slang for e-mail.

Financial innovations have not changed the substance of banking. The core functions of banking
remain the measurement, acceptance and management of risk.

ALAN GREENSPAN
chairman, Federal Reserve Board

About the author

Warren Edwardes is Chief Executive of Delphi Risk Management, a London-based financial instrument innovation, communication and risk management consultancy. He has over 20 years of first-hand experience in the financial markets. Prior to founding Delphi, he was on the board of Charterhouse Bank as Director, Financial Engineering in the Capital Markets Division. He has also worked for the Equitable Life Assurance Society, the UK Government Actuary's Department and the treasuries of Barclays Bank, British Gas and Midland Bank. Whilst an undergraduate in Probability, he applied his training by working in a betting shop. He is Director of the London International School of Banking and, until recently, was visiting professor at the Korea Banking Institute.

Warren Edwardes has designed and implemented numerous innovative financing, investment and derivative structures since 1978, including the break forward, limit swap and perpetual swap and this book includes the story behind some of his inventions. His wide range of publications includes 'Derivatiphobia' and 'How to capture the big new IDEA'. In innovation management, he coined the concept 'hindervation' which helps firms to remove innovation roadblocks or creativity crashers and also encourages innovation through 'upside-down thinking' and 'cross-thinking'. He is often invited to present his 'IDEA kit'.

Besides his conventional academic training in Probability at Sheffield University, and then Economics and Econometrics at Southampton University, Warren Edwardes was schooled in communication at the London Academy of Performing Arts and is an Advanced Toastmaster and a Past-President of a Toastmasters International club, the worldwide public speaking organization.

He is a frequent conference chairman and speaker on a range of banking and financial topics in many countries and has often appeared on television.

Following a negotiating course, Warren Edwardes once complained about his hotel room in pursuit of a discount. He did not get a free room at the Barcelona Ritz, but a year later married Esperanza, the chain's Head of Quality Control. He's stopped complaining!

Exchanges of ideas and experiences are most welcome. Warren Edwardes can be contacted with details of financial instruments omitted or any comments. Also contact Delphi for free derivatives software. Amendments, comments and Frequently Asked Questions to this, the first edition of *Key Financial Instruments* will be posted on to the WebPage: www.dc3.co.uk/kfi.htm

Delphi's e-mail: kfi@dc3.co.uk

Delphi's website: www.dc3.co.uk

Contents

The Big Why

In Holland in the 1630s there was a lively options market in tulip bulbs – until the wife of a trader cooked a bulb thinking it was an onion. Has much changed?

In the late 1990s the 'hedge fund', Long Term Capital Management, received a USD3.5 billion bailout. And this firm was founded in 1994 with two Nobel laureates. Soon afterwards, NatWest bank was criticized over their GBP77 million option mispricing loss. Such events suggest that there is still a great deal for bankers, regulators and corporations to understand about derivatives.

But on 10 April 1999, the *Financial Times* reported that 'Assurers may face GBP14 billion bill for pension guarantees'. The losses could have been mitigated through using derivatives and dwarf those that arose through using derivatives.

And the *Financial Times* reported on 15 September 1999 that 'US prosecutors have charged Martin Armstrong, chairman of offshore investment group Princeton Economics International, with securities fraud in connection with the sale of USD3 billion in bonds to foreign investors'. Princeton Economics was yet another 'hedge fund' that did the opposite – it carried out futures markets operations to *take* risk.

I met six honest serving men. They taught me all I know. Their names were – Who, What and Why; Where, When and How.

RUDYARD KIPLING

Just as this book was being finalized, Stephen Byers, the UK Department of Trade and Industry Minister, held a summit with chairmen of British mortgage banks to discuss lending practices and terms. Many bank chairmen declined the invitation. According to *The Times* of 23 October 1999 a bank source said 'inviting the chairmen of the country's mortgage lenders indicated a profound misunderstanding of how mortgage lenders work . . . chairmen would not be conversant with the finer details of specific products'. Sadly, it may be wrong to assume that bank chairmen do not understand what happens in the banks under their charge. But the quoted proud statement perhaps suggests something worse. Obtaining a broad understanding of relatively simple products such as fixed rate mortgages and their embedded derivatives and talking to a briefing is deemed to be beneath the dignity of some senior bankers and best left to jolly good chaps on the dealing desks. It is no wonder that bank after bank loses a small fortune on derivatives trading.

This book brings financial instruments to life. It clears away the cobwebs, identifies and explains not only the Who? What? Where? When? and How? of financial product development but most importantly, Why? Thus the reader will gain an understanding of not only customers' needs-driven solutions but also bankers' bonus-driven schemes. And through history, apply these techniques to future financial instruments.

Foreword

I first met Professor Warren Edwardes more than a decade ago, when we both joined the newly formed capital markets division of a British merchant bank. Professor Edwardes was at the leading edge of a new breed of bankers, bearing the weighty title of Chief Financial Engineer. Never having encountered a 'financial engineer' before, I was initially intimidated, but soon learned the value of having so much brainpower dedicated to helping solve my clients' problems.

At the time, Professor Edwardes was undoubtedly the leading derivatives innovator in Britain; although many have moved the technology forward since then, many of the developments have built on his pioneering ideas. He taught me two important lessons which also flow through this book:

- most new instruments are simply variations on a theme and therefore not nearly as mysterious as they might initially appear; and

- innovation should deliver real value, and not additional unwanted risk, to the client.

I relied on Professor Edwardes to assist with a wide range of client issues, from tax strategies to economic exposures, all of which he tackled with enthusiasm and a great deal of useful lateral thinking. Indeed, the annual reports of some of the world's largest companies feature his innovative solutions. Professor Edwardes is a dynamo of good ideas, which fill the pages of this book.

Professor Edwardes has continued his extraordinary career, advising clients throughout the world on the management of risk. This book benefits from this long experience but equally importantly it is a lot like him – somewhat irreverent and always approachable. This is a book, then, for all risk managers, in corporations and financial institutions, whether new to the markets or needing to freshen their knowledge. I can promise you that it will be an informative and enjoyable read, a combination not usually found in financial books!

Janine Peake, Director, Investment Banking, Bankers Trust Company. *Ms Peake is a Member of Council for the UK Association of Corporate Treasurers, and the Chairman of the ACT's Editorial Committee.*

Preface

The international financial markets have seen a plethora of products over the last two decades. Many of them have gained a great deal of publicity but found little customer demand. Ultimately a good instrument is one that sells repeatedly, meeting a genuine customer requirement. Nevertheless, complex tailormade products developed can raise the profile of a bank and generate plain vanilla or standard unstructured business.

Part I sets the scene, providing an introduction to the world of financial instruments and derivatives, some thoughts on how to capture new ideas and on what drives financial instrument innovation. Markets are not as global as they seem and the development process does not always spread from developed to emerging markets – Chapter 2, How to capture the big new IDEA, covers an ingenious mortgage product developed in South Africa in 1993. It was only launched in the UK with great fanfare in 1998.

Part II looks at some key financial instruments seen in the development of the financial markets derivatives. This part is not designed to be exhaustive as dozens of books have covered the same ground, but provides a sufficient background to the following parts of the book. However, it covers the key financial instruments of forwards, futures, swaps and options as applied to the management of risk in interest rates, currencies, equity, commodities and inflation and looks at the construction of hybrid products using building blocks. Part II is rounded off with a brief look at capital market products and an in-depth analysis of derivatives for the retail client.

In Part III, I present two case studies on the break forward and perpetual swaps, financial products I developed in the 1980s. The entire innovation process is described from concepts to creativity to communication and closing. There are very few genuine new financial products. Many products developed more than a decade ago are now finding themselves being re-invented. The product featured in the first case study, the break forward was re-invented in 1998. Amazingly this was done by the very same bank that originally created it.

Part IV on risk management includes hedge choice and performance measurement, a substantial chapter on legal risk management by Iona Levine, who set up and heads the derivatives legal practice at Hammond Suddards and a chapter on the taxation aspects of derivatives and risk management.

Part V looks at current developments and trends, featuring the new developments of credit derivatives and insurance derivatives, and also includes Chapter 13, Dangers and disasters; profits and principles', which looks at financial market ethical issues. The part closes with some crystal ball gazing at likely developments and a concluding section, '*Less technophilia – have faith in fools*'.

Derivatives were first constructed as a means of hedging risk. In fact they were known as 'hedging' or 'risk management' products developed before the 'D' word was coined in the mid-1980s. It is natural, therefore, for me to include as Appendix 1, 'Financial risk types'. Appendix 2 is 'Financial risk management instruments.' The list is not simply a dry shopping-list of financial products. It is an opinionated commentary with words of warning on these key instruments. This is not just a book about derivatives. The 'key financial instruments' described here include innovative cash instruments that may or may not have required derivatives in their construction. Appendix 3 is a glossary of 'Risk management terms' used elsewhere in the book or in the markets. Appendix 4 provides a detailed look at Islamic financial products because an objective look at developments in this market illustrates the thought and management processes required in financial instrument innovation.

There are three kinds of lies – lies, damned lies and statistics

---

BENJAMIN DISRAELI

Almost every financial markets book includes statistics on how much business in a certain type of bond or financial market derivative has grown exponentially over the past decade. This book does not contain such meaningless statistics of market volumes. Because of the volume of interbank trading and the fickleness of financial markets, such statistics which purport to measure liquidity cannot be used as a reliable guide to what end-users want to know. *Can I get out of a position at a reasonable price when I want to?* It is worth recalling that trading in derivatives with the London local authorities such as Hammersmith & Fulham also grew exponentially until they came grinding to a halt. And one of my products, the Scout generated several column inches of reporting and is featured in many a financial market dictionary. There was not a single Scout sold. History shows that it is also wise to be careful of official market statistics. There have been cases of interdealer circular transactions designed to inflate reported turnover. One such case I am aware of occurred in 1991. And it did not happen in emerging futures exchanges in Asia or Latin America. It took place in one of the world's major financial centres, London.

So ignore total volume statistics, nearly all of which is interbank and provides little indication of underlying interest and the projected level of liquidity in a particular market required to ensure an orderly exit from a position. When you want to get out of a trade you may find that everybody else may also be rushing for the exit.

This book will assist finance directors and corporate treasurers who are at the receiving end of sales pitches by structured derivatives marketers. It will help senior bankers to re-charge their creative force and help them to recognize past developments rather than re-invent wheels. It will clarify ideas perhaps not fully understood. Finance students and new bankers in their understanding of the financial instrument development process will also find this book useful, as will corporate and personal bankers and financial advisers who advise on products with embedded derivatives such as guaranteed investments or rate capped loans. Finally, all business-men and business students will enhance their understanding of the creativity process in, arguably, the most innovative sector of the economy.

On a point of style, the masculine form is used for clarity rather than exclusion. *He* is used rather than alternating between *he* and *she* or using the inelegant *s/he*.

It is important to clarify that this book offers generic insights and broad strategies, rather than specific investment, financing, taxation or legal advice. For such advice, the reader is strongly advised to consult a professional adviser.

Warren Edwardes, Serinyà, Girona, Spain

Introduction

At the end of 1998, financial markets were concerned about the smooth introduction of the euro. At the end of 1999, as the last millennium drew to a close, many were hoarding cans of food in anticipation of a Y2K computer meltdown. Personally, I chose not to travel by aeroplane early in the New Year. But even with the Y2K fear out of the way, *Derivatiphobia* will surface several times a year as a bank or corporation loses money through derivatives.

Part I provides an approachable introduction to the world of financial instruments and derivatives, clearing away some of the mystique and jargon. In order to understand financial market innovation, I follow with some thoughts on how to capture big new ideas and on what drives financial instrument innovation. Is financial market innovation largely 'ignorance innovation', or to put it bluntly 'ripping off the technically less competent'? Markets are not as global as they seem, and the development process does not always spread from developed to emerging markets. This part covers an ingenious mortgage product developed by one of my clients in South Africa in 1993. It was only launched in the UK with great fanfare in 1998.

A couple of the people who were in the core places within Barings that should have been administering a high level of control . . . had what I would describe as almost no understanding of the fundamentals of the business.

NICK LEESON,

interview with David Frost, British Broadcasting Corporation

Introduction to the world of financial instruments and derivatives

'Derivatiphobia'

Millenniumitis, the state of being in fear of the supposed catastrophic things that will happen when the calendar clicks over to the new century will be an extinct fear by the end year 2000. However, *Derivatiphobia*, the spine-chilling fear of anything associated with the 'D' word has reached epidemic proportions and shows no sign of disappearing. Recently released from prison, twenty-something Nick Leeson brought *Derivatives* to the front page of every newspaper in February 1995 with losses of USD1400 million. And in October 1998, UBS AG Chairman Mathis Cabiallavetta and other top officials at Europe's biggest bank resigned. This followed the 950 million Swiss franc charge UBS was forced to take for its derivatives and investment exposures to so-called 'hedge fund' Long Term Capital Management. Note that the 'hedge fund' was started in 1994 and with two Nobel laureates in their management team. There is clearly still a great deal for bankers, regulators and corporations to understand about derivatives.

And it is not only UBS that has suffered. NatWest was criticized for their GBP77 million loss through the mis-pricing of interest rate options. The blind faith accorded to computer outputs is touching but misplaced. The *Financial Times*, commenting on the NatWest loss in its editorial rightly stated that 'computers cannot substitute for the vigilance of good people'. A financial engineer worth hiring is intelligent enough to out-smart his management accounting/bonus system, particularly if management does not appreciate the differences between its various lines of business. In 'No cowboy atmosphere here', 14 March 1997, the *Financial Times* quoted Martin Owen, NatWest Market's then chief executive as saying that 'interest rate swaps are a standard part of any bank treasury operation'. Quite true. But NatWest's difficulty arose from the mis-pricing of interest rate options, another standard but quite different instrument. The FT's Lex column of the same day stated that 'interest rate and currency options . . . are standard banking products. NatWest has been using them for a decade to hedge fixed rate mortgages'. Interest rate options? I can imagine how such options can be used to protect a mortgage lender during the offer stage or in the event of an early repayment by a borrower. But I was surprised to read that NatWest had apparently been using currency options to hedge fixed rate mortgages!

But have no illusions. Derivatives are not going to be swept under the carpet. This book takes a fresh look at financial derivative instruments, clearing away the myths surrounding the subject. You may have read that Mr Leeson was writing those infamous 'straddles'. Many of Barings' former shareholders perhaps feel that 'strangles' would have been an appropriate antidote to such apparently dangerous exotic products.

Perhaps responsible for derivatiphobia has been the plethora of seemingly unrelated products. The hitherto arcane subject of financial products has, arguably, more than its fair share of jargon. Take, for example, a 'knockout' and a 'straddle'.

So do you think you know the difference between them? Too embarrassed to ask?

Well, they were both seen at the Rome Olympics. A 'straddle' was the standard technique for the high jump at the time and the knockout was used by the then Cassius Clay to close his positions.

Never be afraid to ask the simplest of questions – and persist until YOU understand the answer. Any 'loss of face' suffered will be a lot less painful than the serious financial consequences of entering into sexy but inappropriate products. It is hardly surprising that disasters have occurred. A senior manager in the treasury department of a Top 5 British corporation said: *'neither our board nor our auditors understand what they've been told'*.

Neither a borrower nor a lender be

Shakespeare wrote in *Hamlet*, 'Neither a borrower nor a lender be'. No doubt he was looking forward to an explosion in off-balance sheet 'derivative' products some 400 years later.

The recent spate of derivatives disasters in Asia as well as in nearly every corner of the globe has led to a fear more paralyzing than that of flying or indeed of spiders. Derivatiphobia has replaced arachnophobia in the psychiatrist's office. Perhaps it is the mystique surrounding the subject? Newspapers have reported on losses at a number of prominent consumers or buyers of derivatives. Large corporations such as Procter & Gamble and Metallgesellschaft, or local governments such as Orange County in California and Hammersmith and Fulham in London are amongst the organizations that have apparently lost money through derivatives. But derivatives losses have also extended to the providers of derivatives. Many such banks such as Barings, Union Bank of Switzerland and NatWest Bank have either been taken over by others or undergone major restructuring following derivatives disasters.

The link between derivatives losses and bankers'

> *'The recent spate of derivatives disasters in Asia as well as in nearly every corner of the globe has led to a fear more paralyzing than that of flying or indeed of spiders.'*

difficulties may, of course, be pure coincidence. In fact Marc Ospel, SBC's chief executive was quoted in the *Financial Times* of 25 May 1998 as saying that UBS's derivatives losses were a '*fraction of their annual revenue power in this area*'. Although banks and corporations have made larger losses through standard plain vanilla loans, or through interest rate or currency exposures *not hedged*, derivatives have generated such a bad press that internal and external supervisors have placed tighter controls on such instruments than perhaps justified by their risk and reward. But unlike loans, derivatives can lead to losses far higher than the cash put upfront. Whilst lenders are often tempted to lend further sums to borrowers in distress, derivatives usually involve unlimited liability. Large losses can mount up without the ability, or perhaps willingness, to close the position. To further quote Mr Ospel in the same interview with the *Financial Times*, 'In this business, where decisions of significant size and impact are taken within minutes, obviously you have to delegate significant authority. This requires a high level of confidence in the professionals responsible.'

The term 'derivative' is quite familiar now. But I had not heard of it a decade ago. In 1987 I went through a series of interviews at a US bank in London. I was delighted when the job offer letter arrived. 'Head of Derivatives' was the position. But I had a problem. I had been dealing with foreign exchange, futures, swaps and options since the late 1970s. But what on earth were these 'derivatives' that I was going to head up? The term was unknown to me. It was an American bank so I checked American usage.

Webster's *Ninth New Collegiate Dictionary* (1987) made no mention of financial instruments in its definition. Webster's defined *derivative* thus:

1. A word formed by derivation;

2. Something derived;

3. The limit of the ratio of the change in a function to the corresponding change in its independent variable as the latter change approaches to zero;

4. (a) A chemical substance related structurally to another substance and theoretically derivable from it. (b) A substance that can be made from another substance in one or more steps.

At the time in London, the financial products that we now call 'derivatives' were referred to as 'hedging instruments'. Just as a Minister for Defence has been known to order his armed forces to attack, these hedging instruments have been used as vehicles for speculation to the cost of the shareholders or taxpayers of many an institution. In fact, hedge funds unashamedly use hedging instruments to take a position in the market. On 16 September 1992, George Soros made a billion dollars. He had successfully speculated against sterling, and the pound duly fell sharply after its withdrawal from the European Exchange Rate Mechanism. Soros' reported use of currency options to speculate on sterling's fall, repeated in May 1998, was to take on risk. No shrinking violet risk-avoiding hedger he, despite the fact that funds such as those under his management are known as 'hedge' funds.

So the use of the word 'derivative' avoids a value judgement on its use. It is instructive to look closely at Webster's definition of 'derivative'.

1. A word formed by derivation? Derivatiphobia certainly falls under such a definition!

2. Something derived? A financial market derivative is indeed a financial instrument that is derived from a cash market or standard or 'plain vanilla' financial market instrument. A cash market instrument is a financial market instrument that involves paying a principal sum upfront. For this, the buyer obtains the right to interest and return of principal after a period of time (a loan, deposit or a bond) or for a part ownership of a company (a share).

3. The ratio of the change in a function to the corresponding change in its independent variable? Curiously, this definition of derivative is similar to that ubiquitous Greek symbol delta – δ – an important ratio in the pricing and hedging of options. Delta

is the change in the price of an option on a particular financial instrument, relative to the change in the price of the underlying financial instrument.

4. (a) Are derivatives structurally related to other substances? (b) Can a derivative be made from something else in one or more steps? In answer to question 4b – Yes, most certainly! Financial derivatives can also be derived from a combination of cash market instruments or other derivative instruments. In fact, the vast majority of financial instruments are not revolutionary new instruments. They are merely combinations of older generation derivatives and/or standard cash market instruments. This is the building block approach first used by a number of financial institutions in the late 1980s to explain financial engineering. Back to 4a, we can say that derivatives are structurally related to other substances. This 'structural relation' is driven by financial arbitrage. Although derivatives have taken on a life of their own, their prices are structurally related to the prices of their theoretically constituent parts. This does not mean that a derivative has to be derived or created each and every time it is sold from its various bits and pieces. It is just that efficient financial markets monitor the prices of all the financial components of a treasurer's toolbox and if the price of the derivative is too high then others will step in to manufacture the derivative and undercut the price rather than buy one off-the-shelf. If the price of the packaged product is a bargain, then the derivative will be bought for spare parts that could be sold separately or repackaged to form other derivatives.

> '. . . we can define a . . . derivative . . . as a treasury or capital markets instrument that is derived from or bears a close relation to a cash instrument or another derivative instrument.'

So we can define a financial market derivative instrument as a treasury or capital markets instrument that is derived from or bears a close relation to a cash instrument or another derivative instrument.

So this definition includes the sort of 'new' products that I had been dealing with up to my 'Head of Derivatives' job offer in 1987. The 'new' products that were called hedging or risk management products and included futures, swaps, forward rate agreements, options and interest rate caps, the latter being the product that led to difficulties at Hammersmith and Fulham Local Authority and, a decade later, at NatWest Bank. Clearly these hedging products can be used to eliminate risk or to take on risk.

Derivatives were also known as 'off-balance sheet instruments' in the 1980s. There was no asset or liability to put on the balance sheet as such. These instruments involved contingent assets or liabilities depending on the movement of market prices. At that time, transactions and positions in swaps, forwards and options were not recorded on the balance sheet. Such products do not involve the lending or depositing of a principal sum at the time of transaction. Furthermore, there was no requirement to back business in them with capital. They may involve a promise to lend or to exchange currencies some time in the future or provide the right to do so on payment of an insurance premium upfront.

Many of these derivative instruments do not, in fact, involve the delivery of a financial instrument in the future. They are 'contracts for differences'. If it were not for the purposes of avoiding the gambling laws of various countries, such 'financial instruments' would be more honestly called 'bets'. Interest rate futures contracts or FRAs are no less than bets on the future course of a particular interest rating. The price (or implied interest rate) written into the contract is compared with the interest rate outcome at the agreed date or dates in the future and cash is exchanged based on the difference.

There is considerable debate as to whether 'on balance sheet instruments' should be included in the definition of derivatives. Under the 'made from something else' definition of derivatives we should also include the sort of products that brought down Robert Citron of Orange County. He had not been dealing with hedging or risk management instruments. They were not 'off-balance-sheet'. They were not contracts for differences. The Treasurer of Orange County was strictly restricted in their use. He bought bonds that had bets on currencies embedded within them. The bonds were thus derivatives, as they were derived from other financial instruments. The structured bonds he bought were a potent cocktail of ordinary bonds, laced with various cross-currency interest rate swaps. The concoction was volatile and the hangover lasting.

And finally . . .

The 'key financial instruments' described in this book may be complex or simple. They may be used to avoid risk or to speculate. They may be called 'risk management products', 'hedging products', 'off-balance-sheet instruments' or 'derivatives'. But the financial markets have changed considerably over the past 20 years. The simple fixed rate mortgages or equity-market-linked deposits sold by savings banks are manufactured using interest rate swaps or equity options. They are financial derivatives.

We imagine the edge of chaos as a place where there is enough innovation to keep a living system vibrant, and enough stability to keep it from collapsing into anarchy. It is a zone of conflict and upheaval, where the old and the new are constantly at war. Finding the balance point must be a delicate matter – if a living system drifts too close, it risks falling over into incoherence and dissolution; but if the system moves too far away from the edge, it becomes rigid, frozen, totalitarian. Both conditions lead to extinction. Too much change is as destructive as too little. Only at the edge of chaos can complex systems flourish.

MICHAEL CRICHTON,
The Lost World, Alfred A. Knopf, New York, 1995

2

How to capture the big new IDEA

Why creativity?

If you try to do things, sometimes you'll get it wrong. If you execute everybody who tries to do something and gets it wrong, pretty soon you'll have nobody who tries to do anything. That's exactly the wrong way around.

PETER BURT,

chief executive of Bank of Scotland after the collapse of his bank's arrangement with Pat Robertson, controversial US television evangelist, 10 June 1999

There will be always be innovation in the financial system but for an individual established financial institution, 'Why creativity?' is a very good question. Why not just wait for a small competitor to break ranks, introduce a new product, and then replicate it?

But creativity is not about inventing products from scratch. Many useful financial products are in use elsewhere or went out of use perhaps because of regulation or tax considerations. In the late 1980s, Banco Santander and Banco Bilbao Vizcaya trumpeted the 'guerra de supercuentas' or the super-account war. They started to pay interest on current accounts. But Barclays Bank, a relatively small player in the Spanish market had paid interest on such accounts for some time before the 'guerra'! In early 1998, 'current account mortgages' were launched by Virgin Direct in the UK – the Virgin One Account. Some small UK mortgage banks and insurance-company-owned banks also provided such all-in-one accounts. Such accounts blend borrowings and savings, so that any income is used to reduce borrowings, whilst the borrower retains the right to re-borrow up to his pre-agreed limit at will. But despite the hype and gimmicky press conferences, there was absolutely nothing new in such mortgages! Such accounts have been common in South Africa since a client of mine, the Standard Bank of South Africa, introduced the access bond in 1993.

Always waiting for another firm to introduce a product first in a game of catch-up may be fine, but shortsighted, in retail financial products. Plain vanilla or standard financial product expertise is simply not good enough in the capital markets.

The *Financial Times* of 7 July 1999 reported that the directors of Marks and Spencer recently 'locked themselves away for a three-day strategy brainstorm'. So if we agree that we must have more creativity, how best should a firm or individual achieve 'creative thinking'? Individuals in blue jeans, sneakers and pony tails thinking random thoughts? Committees and working parties scheduling brainstorming sessions? Has anything ever useful been produced by such groups? The only things generated by such bodies are sub-committees and think tanks. The way to The Big Idea was in the word itself – IDEA.

The Big IDEA – impossible

I can't imagine why I hadn't seen it before. I who had had the foresight to buy Polaroid at eight and a half!

---

from the film 'Play it again, Sam' by Woody Allen

Picture a young girl in New England. It is her birthday party. Her father is taking photographs. The girl wants to see the pictures NOW. The father thinks: 'Well, why can't she have the pictures now?'

That father was Edward Land, the inventor of the Polaroid camera. So, think like a child. Think like an Innocent. You can have that picture now. Think *Impossible*.

I recall a new entrant to a dealing room who was forever coming up with scatterbrained ideas. His line management often berated him for not focusing on his day-to-day work on the futures desk. Most of his ideas were indeed off-the-wall, but I was one of the few around to listen to him, and some of his ideas did provide me with a spark of inspiration. Of course I took all the credit, and he was soon fired for not concentrating on the job at hand! The reverse had happened to me a number of times, and the phenomenon of idea theft was a feature in the book *Liar's Poker* (Michael Lewis, Hodder & Stoughton, 1989).

'There's no use trying, one can't believe impossible things', said Alice. 'I daresay you haven't had much practice. Why sometimes I've believed six impossible things before breakfast', said the Queen.

LEWIS CARROLL

in *Alice in Wonderland*

There was a novel advertisement by a job seeker in the September 1998 issue of *Director* magazine. 'Court Jester. Ageing manager seeks appointment as court jester or fool to chief executive of large public company. Will provide own bladders and fool's cap.' Ridiculous? Absolutely not. The idea was that centuries ago, kings who were surrounded by yes-men and sycophants had fools who had licence to ridicule policies without fear of losing their heads. Present day chief executives are also surrounded by yes-men. They need someone to give them an honest opinion. Someone has to tell the emperors of the boardrooms that they are not wearing any clothes before disasters strike.

I would venture to suggest that the reason for the demise of Asian economies such as Korea was not because of a low level of education. Just the opposite is the case. Economics PhDs and university professors have dominated recent governments. Korea fell because of the strict hierarchical system and respect for elders. There was a shortage of fools brave enough to point out the obvious. 'But Mr Bank President, should this bank be lending so many times its capital base to this *chaebol*?' Allow your staff to help you break the mould and think the impossible.

The Big IDEA – disasters

Remember the two benefits of failure. First, if you do fail, you learn what doesn't work; and second, the failure gives you the opportunity to try a new approach.

ROGER VON OECH

Now let us move to a glue laboratory. The scientist is trying to produce super-glue. But he tries and tries and the glue just does not stick. The product is a complete disaster. Have you ever heard of glue that does not stick? Well, you have it in every office in the world. The scientist at 3M had inadvertently invented the Post-it note. Disasters are sometimes opportunities. The Post-it note is everywhere and is the most profitable product at 3M.

A decade ago at Midland Bank's Treasury we created, on the

back of apparent customer demand, a tender-to-contract currency exposure contract. I did not really think it would fly for a number of reasons, but called it the SCOUT – shared currency option under contract. Midland gained considerable publicity and several news column inches after the launch. To this date, however, not a single SCOUT has been sold, but awareness of Midland's ingenuity and customer service was enhanced and plain vanilla currency options were sold! The SCOUT is, nevertheless, still featured in numerous *Dictionaries of Finance*. As it did not cost a penny to produce and no brochures were printed, in terms of public relations generated the SCOUT may be the most profitable financial product ever launched! So disasters have silver linings.

The Big IDEA – everywhere

It is always at Perpignan station, when Gala is making arrangements for the paintings to follow us by train, that I have my most unique ideas.

SALVADOR DALÍ
in *Diary of a Genius*

Let us now move across to a forest in the Jura Mountains in France. It is wartime 1941. A scientist is out hunting with his dog. When he gets home, he finds that wood-burs have stuck to his woollen jacket and trousers and to his dog's coat.

He decides to examine them. Carefully inspecting the burs under a microscope, he finds hundreds of little hooks engaging the loops in the material and fur.

The scientist, George de Mestral, makes a machine to duplicate the hooks and loops in nylon. He calls his new product 'Velcro', from the French words *VELours* and *CROchet*.

The rest is history. Today there are thousands of uses of Velcro fasteners from rucksacks to clothing, all thanks to a man hunting with his dog in the mountains.

So, think *everywhere*. Think when out walking. Think when in the shower. Think when listening to a boring speaker. Just switch off and think about that problem that has been bugging you.

One of Honda's most original sportscar designs, the NSX supercar, is reputed to have been sketched by Nobuhiko Kawamoto, the President of Honda, whilst doodling during a tedious board meeting.

The latest in the hugely popular Harry Potter series of 'children's' books was launched on 8 July 1999. Its author, J. K. Rowling, revealed how she came across her ideas. Sometimes they just came like magic, and other times she had to sit and think for about a week before she managed to work out how something would develop. The idea for Harry Potter actually came whilst she was travelling on a train, and it just 'popped' into her head. It was the most interesting train journey she'd ever taken. By the time she'd got out of the train, many of the characters in the books had already been invented.

I was once attending an extremely tediously presented seminar on corporation tax, when my mind wandered to solve a problem a corporate customer was having with currency translation exposure. My lack of concentration led to the creation of the perpetual currency swap!

So do think everywhere. And, again, don't bother with those contrived brainstorming sessions and working parties! You cannot plan to create on demand. But you can organize your mind to be constantly receptive to new ideas wherever you happen to be.

The big IDEA – archive

It is unforgivable in the course of a meeting or conversation to let ideas float away un-captured, to be lost for all time, when so little effort and so simple a device (a notebook) can preserve them and bring them back to mind later.

RICHARD BRANSON,

in a speech to an Institute of Directors annual conference

The problem, however, with thinking everywhere is that thoughts are often forgotten until somebody else thinks of them. It is then much too late! So, write it down. Archive that thought. Keep a pen and paper handy in every room of the house, especially by your bed and near the shower! What about when you are driving? Forget the pen and paper. Have a dictaphone in the car. Archive those thoughts – NOW.

Many of us have come across situations where we have proposed ideas in brainstorming meetings or around a coffee machine or even directly to the boss, only to find that someone a good deal more senior grabs the credit. I proposed fixed-rate mortgages at my bank with hedging through interest rate swaps in 1986. They were new in the UK, but common in the US. The idea was dismissed. Six months later, after I had moved from product development to another unit, my bank began marketing fixed rate mortgages with great fanfare. I was naïve enough to think that I should have got some credit for the idea! In 1993, years after the innocent futures dealer was sacked, and well before knowledge management became fashionable, I developed an innovation management system for a client, the Delphi Thought Pad. This allowed anyone from receptionist to internal auditor to input thoughts even in their pre-idea stage on to a database and generate a discussion. Some people are good at ideas whilst others excel at implementing. The advantage, furthermore, is that others cannot steal the ideas of the newcomer. At bonus time, reward is given where it is due. Every contributor in the team or even outside the team takes credit as input and dates are recorded.

However full 'information-sharing' is not always advisable. In cultures such as Korea, loyalty can be to university or school alumni rather than to the firm. The *Economist* of 3 July 1999 reported that 'sharing information with Korean employees can easily backfire because most of them gossip over drinks with friends who work for competitors.' The article quoted Dave Parker, president of Nestlé Korea which operated an open information system, as being alarmed at the amount of information available to his firm's competitors. In early 1999, Nestlé introduced Taster's Choice coffee packaged with a water container. A mere two weeks after the product was launched, a local competitor began selling its own copy. But perhaps this particular case was all down to local language difficulties? After all in Korea, 'coffee' is commonly pronounced 'copy'. There is also the problem caused by staff leaving for competitor banks. If full information on work-in-progress is made available to all, then staff about to leave will scan the system before resigning and structure the products for their new firm. This happened with one of the financial products I developed. And I must confess that I have re-launched financial products that I developed for previous employers.

The big IDEA – the IDEA kit

He who asks is a fool for five minutes, but he who does not ask remains a fool forever.

Chinese proverb

So to enhance creativity, keep on your desk a simple IDEA kit. It is no more than a bag with a LEGO block, a Post-it note, a strip of Velcro and a golf pencil.

The LEGO block represents *impossible* or *innocence* – think like a child and ask stupid implausible foolish questions. Raw recruits to a firm should be encouraged to ask: 'Why do we do it this way?' If

---

'A solution that does not work for today's problem may be just what you needed for yesterday's unsolved and shelved problem.'

---

management does not have a good answer other than 'When I want your ideas I'll give them to you' or 'We've always done it this way' or something similar, then the process must be changed. New fresh viewpoints should be utilized and be encouraged to question everything and report on their findings to senior management.

The Post-it note was a disaster – the non-sticking super glue! Sometimes the best products arise when solving another problem. A solution that does not work for today's problem may be just what you needed for yesterday's unsolved and shelved problem.

The velcro strip represents the motto: Think everywhere.

Finally, the golf pencil reminds us to archive those precious thoughts. Note that thought in the gym. In the car, use a dictaphone.

No chance

Chance discoveries do not occur by chance. An environment must be nurtured to allow fleeting thoughts, those pre-ideas, to be grasped; then recognized for their potential as ideas; turned into tailormade solutions and then finally developed into products for other customers.

Think cross-markets. Problem-solving ideas can often be captured from other markets or businesses. The most successful products are not those that use high-tech mathematics. The best financial market products are the result of the most simple of ideas – but applied in a fresh way to a completely different business. Banks have grown so large that a number of banks are re-inventing the small entrepreneurial merchant banks of 20 years ago within their banks. They are establishing multi-disciplinary cross-markets groups to include not only rocket-scientists, but also practically minded creative lawyers and accountants.

But the creative process in financial institutions does not stop at the creation of new financial products. In this or any other service industry, creativity must be employed to enhance the delivery process or simply to increase efficiency. The most creative field without doubt is finance. Whilst the morality of some financial schemes may be questionable, lessons can be learned from the creative process.

You can't solve a problem by thinking about it too much. Creativity cannot be planned. Inspiration, by its very nature, often comes to you when you are alone. Perhaps in the shower – just when you do not have a notebook at hand. Good ideas just hit you. Recall Archimedes in the bath shouting out, 'Eureka'. No doubt his modern equivalent financial innovator would yell 'Euroclear'. Perhaps some can innovate through brainstorming, mind-mapping and lateral and objective thinking and all that sort of thing. I just find that the most successful and marketable of ideas are the most obvious ones. There is no better way to hinder innovation than to plan to innovate.

Postscript

Given that genuine new ideas are hard to come by and very difficult to patent, perhaps the quickest way to a new idea is to get it from someone else. Keep your mouth shut and ears open, especially in bars in the City of London or Wall Street. Read the *Financial Times* on the train or the aeroplane. And don't talk in the back seat of a taxi. Your excited deal-talk may well be broadcast to the taxi-driver's paymasters working for a competitor. The idle sentence may just provide a missing ingredient to a new product.

I was on a train to London in 1985. The passenger sitting next to me was reading a report. It was headed 'Lloyds Bank – Product Development Department'. It proved to be fascinating. You should have seen the look on his face when I thanked him and gave him my business card – 'Midland Bank – Head of Product Development'.

> *'. . . the most successful and marketable of ideas are the most obvious ones.'*

There is a bank, which will remain nameless, that is permanently interviewing for staff. If a candidate says something useful, his ideas are recorded. But the talkative candidate is discarded as being untrustworthy. Somehow, keeping quietly mysterious does not help the candidate either. There is, of course, no job on offer!

And beware of the boastful. I have come across an amazing number of financial markets people who proudly boast about their firm's work. I recall a lunch a former bank employer hosted for some investment bankers. We had worked together on a major deal. I was flabbergasted when my show-off boss coolly and calmly told them what we were working on. In my experience the most leaky are the most senior. Perhaps the key to successful innovation is skilful ego-massaging?

As an innovation management consultant, it is not always possible to get a client to sign a written confidentiality agreement. Over the course of a year, I hinted at a structure to a long-standing 'friend', a treasurer of a bank. He said that he really needed to understand the structure, and that I should explain it to him with an oral confidentiality agreement. A week later he advised me that he could not proceed with the advisory contract proposed. I was shocked and felt more than a little naïve a month later when the *Financial Times* reported that his bank had launched my product. So make sure all proposals are in writing – and with a watertight confidentiality agreement or not at all.

And finally . . .

Capturing the big idea is but the first part of innovation. Innovation involves more than creative thinking. Innovation involves the development of ideas into products and services. And those members of a team with creative minds are often not those best equipped to develop the thoughts into products. And *vice versa*. So develop an ideas management methodology and system that utilizes the best abilities of all in the workplace, and win co-operation by giving credit where it is due. As a financial engineer working in a bank, I often found that my products were being sold by my sales and marketing colleagues. They were the ones to get the bonuses. So I just had to close some big deals myself to prove my worth. In mid-1998 I heard Peter Hain, a UK minister being interviewed on the BBC. *'Do tell me about your new idea, minister,'* the interviewer asked. The idea may well have been Peter Hain's, but somehow I doubt it. Surely a government minister (or a chief executive) should be spending his time evaluating and managing ideas generated by his large team. Mr Hain should have said: *'I'd be delighted to tell you but the idea actually came jointly from my researcher, Ms X and civil servant, Mr Y.'*

Six people seated around the walls of a darkened room. In the open middle space is a chair. Who finds it? Those that sat still and philosophized about where chairs are usually placed in rooms? The innovator who would locate it is the one who'd get up, walk and stumble until he discovered it. Nobody ever found anything whilst sitting down. So QED don't be afraid to stumble.

_____

CHARLES KETTERING

What drives innovation?

Ease of entry

In the financial market, the barriers to product development are incredibly low. Unlike in the industrial world, a manufacturer of a financial product such as a fixed-rate mortgage or an inflation-linked deposit product does not have to create the product and stock shelves. Even in the retail financial services, with the product offered at a fixed rate, the bank always has the right to withdraw the offer. There is usually a 'Special Limited Offer' splashed on prominently. The costs of producing a retail product are limited to the costs of stationery, staff training and computer systems.

In the wholesale financial markets, the costs of developing products are even lower. One of the most successful product launches in my experience was that of a currency-option-based structure. The object of the product was to lower the costs for corporations wanting to tender for overseas contracts. Let us consider a group of UK firms bidding separately for a contract in the US.

The theory was that they could buy one currency option to sell US dollars and buy GB pounds and split the costs of the option amongst themselves. This product was the shared currency option under tender, the SCOUT, referred to in the previous chapter. We drew up legal documentation, produced marketing literature and called the press. The product launch successfully generated widespread publicity but not a single SCOUT was sold! I don't believe that any client even asked for a quotation. But so what? Who knows to this day that the product was a complete flop in terms of business generated? But it increased awareness of the bank's capabilities in treasury products and led to standard options business.

Copyright

It is interesting to examine innovation in another industry – the software industry. In some ways the financial product business is quite similar to the software business. They are not capital intensive – they are both ideas-intensive. If Apple or Netscape has a good idea for a way of doing something, then until very recently the business process could not be successfully patented. The software code could be protected and the look and feel, but the basic idea could not. Apple produced graphical user interfaces (GUIs) well before Microsoft's Windows, SuperCalc and Lotus 123 preceded Microsoft's Excel, and Word Perfect had a dominant market share of word-processing well before Microsoft launched Word. In software, the firm that wins is not necessarily the firm that innovates.

'Who knows to this day that the product was a complete flop in terms of business generated?'

So it has been in the world of financial product innovation. In the late 1980s Spanish banks began to pay interest on cheque accounts. The competition was described in war-like terms: as 'La Guerra de Super Cuentas'. Banco Santander was generally credited with having started this 'super account war'. But it was Barclays

Bank that introduced interest on current accounts into its relatively small operation in Spain. Fixed-rate mortgages cannot be patented.

It now appears that financial products can be patented in the US. The business process through which a firm develops, markets and manages a financial product defined by the business process can be patented. This will ensure that the ideas generated by product developers, provided they can be fully formulated, will be protected. I am in the process of patenting two financing schemes, so I cannot yet vouch for the efficacy of this intellectual property protection process.

Six pillars of financial innovation

There are six main pillars of financial innovation:

- competitive innovation
- regulatory innovation
- accounting innovation
- taxation innovation
- religious innovation
- ignorance innovation.

Competitive innovation

The largest institutions in any industry are often not the leaders in the early-stages of innovation. In the words of the slogan that never was: 'We're number one. Why try harder?' It is the second-placed firm that has to say 'We try harder' to paraphrase the Avis' slogan countering Hertz's 'We're number one'.

But in a free market with low-cost ease of access though the internet, unless firms can develop new financial instruments that meet the changing needs of the marketplace, they will be by-passed. It is no good just being on the right track. If you just stand there, you will be run over.

So competitive innovation seeks to provide a firm's clients with better solutions to its problems. Banks thereby hope to generate a higher market share or a higher profit through satisfying the customer's needs – the famously touted 'needs-driven approach'. I came across a bank marketing director who religiously stuck to this approach and proudly stated that he never mentioned products to customers. At the end of the day, a bank's marketing team has to provide a customer with a product or a service.

I would hazard to say that of the six pillars of financial innovation, this is the most difficult and rarest. There is no free lunch here and margins are slim with such innovation. But unsurprisingly the other forms of financial innovation described below are dressed up for customer consumption to look like competitive innovation.

Regulatory innovation

The eurobond market was created in London by the London merchant bank, S. G. Warburg as a result of two main forces. Firstly, there were regulatory restrictions and fiscal impositions in the United States. Secondly, because of the cold war, the USSR was not keen to invest its funds in the US. A relatively free eurobond market was developed in London for borrowers and investors who wished to avoid US controls.

In 1978 I got my first job in the balance sheet management department of a major British bank. At that time there were very strict quantitative controls on bank lending in the UK. The growth in interest-bearing eligible liabilities (IBELs) was controlled with strict penalties imposed by the Bank of England on banks that exceeded permitted growth. Several regulatory arbitrage schemes were employed to maintain bank lending but avoid paying penalties. The bank loaned money through bankers acceptances, which if sold on did not count as IBELs. Lending was also done through the bank's Paris branch. Such offshore lending even denominated in sterling did not count for IBELs. And where possible lending was carried out between 'make-up days', the dates on which the monthly balance sheets were drawn up for Bank of England reporting purposes. This was to such an extent that the bank's IBELs used to fall after the make-up days by as much as 30 per cent. My bank was the only UK bank that did not have penalties imposed on it.

Regulatory innovation could also include products such as credit derivatives and insurance derivatives. There is a grey area between insurance and banking and the treatment of similar instruments is quite different between them. It pays to be able to choose to book structures in either an insurance company or bank on a case-by-case basis.

A number of products have also been targetted specifically at fund managers with tight regulatory controls. Many such managers are not authorized to use derivatives. But they can buy investments with built-in derivatives structures to provide them with the gearing and risk pattern they seek. Such products were designed specifically for some highly regulated investment funds. In some cases individual institutional investors have bought entire issues of highly geared bonds.

> *'It pays to be able to choose to book structures in either an insurance company or bank on a case-by-case basis.'*

Accounting innovation

The break forward featured later was a case of both accounting innovation and taxation innovation. Finance directors were reluctant to pay currency option premiums upfront. After all, they did not have to do so for standard forward exchange contracts. So I developed the break forward out of a currency option with no explicit option premium. The premium was embedded in the packaged product which consisted of two contracts – a forward contract at a rate worse than market and a 'free' option to unwind. The cash value of the difference between the two contracts amounted to the future value of the option premium. Corporate treasurers knew what they were doing and understood that they were buying options. This was fully explained to them. But the break forward structure was easier to explain to boards of directors who had been comfortable with forwards. A case of accounting innovation.

Taxation innovation

The two case studies featured in Chapters 7 and 8 on the break forward and the perpetual swap both were largely tax-driven innovations. It is all very well coming up with solutions to customer problems, but unless a third party (the taxman) is contributing to the pot, the profitability of deals is often insufficient to justify the effort.

Zero coupon bonds and deep discounted securities were initially tax-driven products in addition to their portfolio immunization benefits. In most jurisdictions, capital gains was generally until fairly recently taxed much more favourably, if taxed at all, than income. Interest was converted into capital gains by various methods. Such schemes are no longer tax-efficient.

Taxation innovation is on the wane as many jurisdictions now have the right to retrospectively tax what they deem to be tax avoidance schemes.

Religious innovation

Religious innovation here largely refers to Islamic banking. There is a comprehensive section on Islamic financial products in Appendix 4 which looks at various creative schemes used to meet the stipulations of the Koran. But there have been a great number of such financial instruments that have only paid lip-service to such objectives.

Islamic banking is more than the prohibition of interest. In conventional banking terms, it is about the introduction of a no pain, no gain system of banking or venture capital investment. But the vast majority of Islamic banking schemes amount to converting interest into capital gains. The processes here were very similar to the tax minimization schemes involving interest elimination. Fifteen years ago, zero coupon bonds and treasury bills were acceptable.

Whilst these instruments are no longer Islamically acceptable, other interest into capital gains structures leaving no risk to the investor are still acceptable.

> *'Ignorance innovation is plain and simple "ripping-off" of customers, not through any fraud or misrepresentation, but through creative financial engineering.'*

Religious innovation is not just limited to Islamic banking. Many non-Islamic countries have usury laws to control maximum interest rates payable by consumers. And recently a number of ethical investment funds have been created to channel funds into firms not dealing with items such as tobacco, alcohol and armaments.

Ignorance innovation

As stated above, competitive innovation seeks to generate new customer solutions through a 'needs-driven' approach. But what is often not obvious is that the 'needs' referred to are those of the bank traders and directors' bonuses rather than those of their customers. Ignorance innovation is plain and simple 'ripping-off' of customers, not through any fraud or misrepresentation, but through creative financial engineering. And the customer may be perfectly happy with the product and the excess profit engineered may well be opportunity profit. If the customer knew how to structure such deals for itself, then it would have obtained a much better package price for the structure.

Sometimes the ignorance may apply not to the corporate treasurer doing the deal but to his superiors. Such innovation falls under 'accounting innovation'.

Some recent public cases where customers have discovered that they have been victims of ignorance innovation are featured in Chapter 13, 'Dangers and disasters; profits and principles'.

Perpetual floating rate notes were issued by banks in the mid 1980s. FRNs traditionally had maturities between five years and 15 years. Naturally, they did not count as primary capital in the same way as did retained earnings or shareholders' funds. So banks issued FRNs but with no maturity date. The structure was akin to preference shares but with floating rates. There was no obligation to repay the 'loans' at any time. The ability of an investor to realize his investment crucially depended on an active and liquid secondary market. And this was limited, as banks that held other banks' perpetual FRNs found that their capital base was reduced by regulators in line with their holdings of such 'perps'. Gradually the true nature of these perps dawned upon investors. They had bought bank liability instruments that they believed were almost like deposits, but paying 25 basis points over LIBOR. As investors stormed out of positions in the perpetual FRNs, prices crashed within days to 80 per cent of the par value they had been trading. The yield was now a more reasonable but still low 250 basis points over LIBOR for bank equity. A case of what appeared to be regulatory innovation was really ignorance innovation.

And finally . . .

Of the six types of financial innovation it would be nice to think that genuine needs-driven competitive innovation was the most common. Regulatory innovation will no doubt continue. Accounting innovation will depend on performance management systems. It is much more easy to generate accounting profits than real profits and every competent financial engineer is capable of manipulating his management accounts. Religious innovation which include ethical innovation is increasing, as Western banks provide Islamic financial instruments, and retail investors increasingly seek 'green' investments. Ignorance innovation will always be around but to a much lower degree. Corporations and retail investors are increasingly likely to cry 'foul' and take banks to court. Even if there is a settlement out of court or the bank wins the case, any whiff of sharp practice can seriously damage a bank's reputation.

The key financial instruments

I lifted the veil of mystery surrounding financial derivatives in Part I and covered the *Why* of financial instrument innovation, outlining the driving forces behind financial market innovation, with a look at the creative thought process.

Part II continues the *Why* theme and examines some of the major risks faced by users of derivatives or products created using derivatives and goes on to look at *What* the core derivatives are. This part looks closely at some key financial instruments seen in the development of the financial markets derivatives. It is not designed to be exhaustive as dozens of books have covered the same ground, but provides a background to the following parts of the book. I cover the key financial instruments of forwards, futures, swaps and options as applied to the management of risk in interest rates, currencies, equity, commodities and inflation and look at the construction of hybrid products using building blocks. Part II is rounded off with a brief look at capital market products and an indepth analysis of derivatives for the retail client. An exhaustive answer to *Why* and *What* in the form of a list of financial risk types and a list of financial instruments is contained in Part V.

Key risks

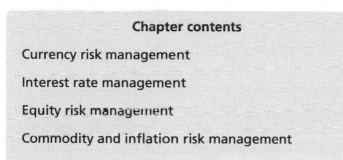

Chapter contents

Currency risk management

Interest rate management

Equity risk management

Commodity and inflation risk management

Derivatives were derived either to hedge or to eliminate risks or to do the opposite – take risks. In fact hedge funds such as Princeton Global Management, the fund which ceased trading in September 1999 amid accusations of fraud, do anything but hedge. They deliberately take risks through futures markets to generate higher returns. So what sort of risks are usually managed by using financial derivatives? This chapter examines the main economic and business risks facing an organization which require immunization.

Currency risk management

Ignoring the 'derivatives' used by the ancient Egyptians, Greeks, Romans and the Dutch tulip dealers often quoted in histories of derivatives, modern financial risk management begins following the collapse of the era of fixed exchange rates and the gold standard. The process accelerated with the global liberalization of foreign exchange controls which in the UK occurred with Margaret Thatcher's election at the end of the 1970s. The consequent floating and volatile exchange rates in the UK meant that corporate treasurers had to actively manage the foreign exchange exposure resulting from international trade. The financial instrument used was the forward foreign exchange contract, which was an agreement to exchange a certain principal amount of one currency for a certain amount of another currency at an agreed exchange rate and on a specified future date.

There are three main types of foreign exchange or currency exposure:

● transaction exposure,
● translation exposure and
● economic exposure.

Transaction exposure

Currency transaction exposure arises out of income and expenditure denominated in a foreign currency. It is the risk of depreciation of a foreign currency receivable or the risk of appreciation of a foreign currency payable measured in terms of the home or accounting currency of an entity.

Consider a British car company, Rover, which exports cars to Spain. The cars are offered for sale in Spanish pesetas which since 1 January 1999 are mere denominations of the euro. In this case, transaction exposure is the risk that the euros received through the sale of Rover cars in Spain could depreciate against sterling and thus wipe out the required profit margin or even lead to a loss.

Translation exposure

Transaction exposure arises out of cash flows. Currency transaction exposure is a function of the revaluation of assets and liabilities.

Translation exposure therefore is the risk of depreciation of a foreign-currency-denominated asset or the appreciation of a foreign-currency-denominated liability.

Rover is a British company but it is wholly owned by Germany's BMW. Rover's balance sheet is in sterling (or so I believe) whilst BMW has a balance sheet denominated in D-marks which are, like Spanish pesetas, now denominations of the euro. Even if Rover proves to be profitable in sterling terms, if sterling depreciates against the euro, then the value of the car company, an asset in BMW's books, will fall and BMW would incur a translation loss.

Translation exposure is not just a book-keeping statistic. Real exposure materializes, leading to real cash losses when a foreign currency denominated subsidiary is sold or a currency loan is repaid on maturity. In the early 1980s Laker Airways, a small UK airline, went into liquidation partly through economic exposure. The company had a substantial LIBOR-linked US dollar loan raised to pay for new DC10 aircraft. The airline's year-by-year profitability was dominated by foreign exchange gains, as sterling had appreciated against the US dollar from GBP/USD1.50 to GBP/USD2.40, and so its management was not persuaded by its bankers to hedge the company's translation exposure. Sterling duly fell back from GBP/USD2.40 towards GBP/USD1.50, and the airline not only suffered through higher interest charges in sterling, but also was liable to raise more sterling to pay off its US dollar debts.

'Translation exposure . . . is the risk of depreciation of a foreign-currency-denominated asset or the appreciation of a foreign-currency-denominated liability.'

More recently I was asked for advice by the bursar of an East Asian university on fund raising for a new hospital wing. Foreign exchange borrowing controls were about to be lifted and they said that they were thinking about borrowing in low-cost US dollars rather at much higher domestic interest rates. US dollar borrowing may indeed have cost less in the short-term but had they executed such a strategy, they would have faced a substantial appreciation in their liability when their currency fell in the Asian economic crisis of late 1997.

Economic exposure

If Rover hedges its transaction exposure in EU exports through sales of euros it would lock in the proceeds of its cars in sterling terms. Say the euro appreciates strongly including against sterling. Because of its hedging activity in the foreign exchange market, Rover would not be in a position to pass on the benefit of lower costs in euro terms. Perhaps Saab is a close competitor to Rover in Spain. If the Swedish kronor depreciates against the euro, Saab could be in a position to reduce its prices in euros to euroland and undercut Rover. This is currency economic exposure for Rover. Now if the Swedish kronor does not depreciate against the euro, Rover could still suffer economic exposure in its competition with Saab cars. Saab is a subsidiary of General Motors which owns Vauxhall in the UK. General Motors could switch the production of Saab cars from Sweden to Luton in England which, following the depreciation of sterling, has become a relatively low-cost production base. Recall that Rover has already locked in the value of euros in sterling terms and cannot take advantage of the higher value of the euro. This is also economic currency exposure, also known as 'competitive currency exposure'.

Interest rate management

The tailor of the English playwright Richard Brinsley Sheridan, fed up with his bills not being paid, pleaded, 'At least you can pay me the interest on the principal', which provoked the reply: 'It is not my interest to pay the principal; nor is it my principle to pay the interest'.

In contrast to the UK and other economies which have a substantial international component to their economies, foreign exchange exposure has been of relatively little importance to US treasurers. On the other hand, interest rate management came to the fore when the then chairman of the Federal Reserve Paul Volcker raised US interest rates from about 5 per cent to 21 per cent, and then all the way back down again to 6 per cent in the time span of about a year.

Interest rate exposure is the risk that interest rates will rise leading to a rise in the interest liabilities of borrowers or the risk that interest rates will fall leading to a fall in the interest rate income of floating rate investors. Fixed rate bond investors also have an interest rate exposure as the value of their assets is determined by the present value of the future stream of income from the bonds. As interest rates rise, so do the discounting rates used to calculate the present values and therefore the value of their investments fall.

UK mortgage borrowers have traditionally borrowed for house purchase at floating rates but over the past decade, fixed-rate mortgages have become commonplace. Retail borrowers thereby avoid risk by passing it on to the mortgage banks, who use a variety of derivatives products to hedge the risk in the market.

A particular form of interest rate risk is interest rate basis risk. This applies when a borrower raises finance linked to one market, but hedges in another market in the same currency. The resultant risk between the two markets is basis risk. An example could be borrowing in the US commercial paper market and using LIBOR-linked derivatives.

Equity risk management

The stock price is derivative of performance in the marketplace and not something you act on with financial engineering.

LOU GERSTNER,
CEO, RJR Nabisco, Fortune, 8 February 1993

Equity risk refers to the risk that the share price of a firm will rise or fall. It also refers to the possible change in the market value of a basket of shares. The expected return on equities is considerably greater than the expected return on bonds because of the higher risk. In the event of a liquidation, deposit holders and bond holders are paid before equity holders receive anything. Accordingly, equity investments are considerably more volatile than bond investments or holding assets in bank deposits. However, a number of banks have issued deposit structures which include linking to various stockmarket indices, thus introducing broad-based equity market linking with a view to taking advantage of the historical high growth in the equity market. These are hedged using equity derivatives.

Equity risk also applies to firms that plan to issue shares in the market to raise working capital or to release value for the start-up owners. In 1987, the UK government launched the privatization of BP. But between the announcement of the offer price and the closing of the offer, there was a worldwide crash in stockmarkets – Black Monday intervened.

Commodity and inflation risk management

It's hard enough to get anyone to listen when you mention derivatives, but if you team them up with commodities, people tend to want to run a mile.

Anonymous derivatives trader, *Risk*, January, 1995

Commodity risk management was, perhaps, practised even before the advent of financial risk management. There were active futures markets in oil, gold, copper, and a variety of agricultural products well before futures markets in financial risk.

Pension funds, in particular, have bought instruments linked to inflation so as to be able to meet their inflation-linked liabilities.

Many utilities around the world also require inflation hedging. The annual percentage price increases they negotiate with their regulators are generally a few percentage points above or below inflation. But inflation risk is no longer taken very seriously, given that inflation around the world has fallen to levels of half a century ago.

And finally

The main risks managed by derivatives are currency, interest rate, equity and commodity risks. But there are infinite varieties and combinations of risks that can be derived. Appendix I contains a comprehensive list of risk types many of which can be managed by using financial derivatives. Some of the risks listed in the appendix arise through the use or abuse of financial instruments.

Derivatives by their nature do not introduce risks of a fundamentally different kind or of a greater scale than those [risks] already present in the financial markets.

PAUL VOLCKER,
former Federal Reserve Chairman

Key financial instruments

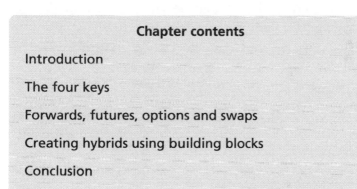

Chapter contents

Introduction

The four keys

Forwards, futures, options and swaps

Creating hybrids using building blocks

Conclusion

Introduction

This chapter provides the key to understanding and practising financial product development. It not only explains how such products have been built from four gene pools, but that an understanding of this process provides the basic recipe for creating an infinite variety of financial products. So read this chapter and go create your own financial product. And I hope you find buyers for it. I wanted to make this book entertaining and avoid technical diagrams. If you really need some pretty pictures, buy one of the fine books listed in Appendix 5. Alternatively, send me an e-mail, I'll draw some and upload it on to the internet. My e-mail address and the URL for updates are given on page x.

The four keys

There are four key financial instruments that can be combined in various forms with each other or with various guises of themselves to form all other financial products. These key products are the spot contract, the forward contract, the option contract and the deposit contract.

Other than a small number of highly exotic financial instruments, most of which I would argue to be of limited end-user use other than perhaps as examples of accounting innovation or ignorance innovation, every financial instrument already created or likely to be created can be broken down into combinations of these key instruments. So a genuine understanding of these simple products is all that is needed. Just go through the list of financial instruments in Appendix 2. They are all built up from these four key instruments.

The first key financial instrument is the spot contract which is a contract to buy or sell some commodity for a cash payment in a particular currency or to exchange one currency for another. Settlement takes place in two business days from the date of dealing in the case of foreign exchange spot contracts. But this is not a derivative contract. Derivatives are derived from this key financial instrument.

'If a product can't be explained, don't permit it until it can.'

Beyond the spot contract, there are two key types of financial instrument which apply to all of the risk types mentioned in the previous chapter: forwards and options. These contracts may be over-the-counter (OTC), which means between a corporate and a bank or bank to bank or exchange-traded. Such exchange-traded forward contracts are known as futures contracts.

The final of the four key financial instruments is the deposit contract. Obviously a loan contract is the same as a deposit, as one party's loan is another party's deposit. With this contract one can perform time shifts, moving cash flows from the beginning of the contract to the end or smoothing out cash flows from a series of contracts to produce an average flat rate for a package.

If it is not clear what an option 'straddle' is or you confuse it with a 'strangle', don't feel intimidated. They are both combinations of easily explained options and you really do not need to know what they are. You need to know WIGO – what is going on. If a product can't be explained, don't permit it until it can. If someone wants to sell you a deferred LIBOR setting swap and you don't know why you should buy it – then don't. The salesman will have a very good reason – his needs for a new Ferrari are probably greater than your needs!

Forwards, futures, options and swaps

Forwards

It is a mistake to look too far ahead. Only one link of the chain of destiny can be handled at a time.

WINSTON CHURCHILL

A forward contract is a firm commitment to buy or sell something. The contract could be for foreign currency, gold, sugar or oil. A variant on a forward contract is a forward contract for differences (FCFD). This is a forward contract but is settled in cash based on price movements.

Forward exchange contracts

The most common forward contract is a forward foreign exchange contract which is a contract to buy a specified amount of currency A for a specified amount of currency B at a specified date in the future and at a specified exchange rate. The standard and therefore liquid maturity dates for such contracts are one week, one month, two months, three months, six months and 12 months beyond the spot date. Intermediate months and longer-dated contracts are also traded in the more liquid currency pairs. Settlement can also be made before the spot date for value tomorrow or even value today using short date swaps – tom/next and spot/next.

To distinguish these contracts from forward swap contracts, they are known as 'forward exchange outright contracts'.

Forward rate agreements (FRAs)

A forward rate agreement (FRA) is used by corporate treasurers to protect against future short-term interest rate costs (or investment returns).

By entering into an FRA, the parties lock in an interest rate for a stated period of time starting on a future settlement date, based on a specified notional principal amount. The buyer of the FRA enters into the contract to protect itself from a future increase in interest rates. This occurs when a company believes that interest rates may rise and wants to fix its borrowing cost today. The seller of the FRA wants to protect itself from future falls in interest rates. Investors who want to hedge the return obtained on a future deposit use this strategy. FRAs are cash settled by way of a formula and lock in the market component only for the borrowing or investment – LIBOR.

'If you are not sure of the basis of an illiquid currency, then confirm it before dealing.'

Essentially, the difference between the FRA contract rate and the LIBOR settlement rate for the FRA interest period in the currency of the notional principal amount is calculated; then pro-rated by the number of days in the FRA interest period over the year basis for the currency of the notional principal – i.e., 360 or 365 days; then as LIBOR is quoted on the basis of interest paid in arrears on the maturity date, the settlement factor is discounted by LIBOR to the start date, the beginning of the interest period. Finally the settlement factor is multiplied by the notional principal amount in the currency of the contracts. LIBOR in most currencies is on a 360-day basis whilst in sterling it is on a 365-day basis. If you are not sure of the basis of an illiquid currency, then confirm it before dealing. It affects the price.

There is no attached facility to borrow or lend funds, and the FRA does not guarantee a future level of borrowing or deposit. The margin over LIBOR that a particular entity must pay in the market can vary considerably over time. Furthermore, the LIBOR defined under the FRA contract may not be the same as the LIBOR defined in the borrower's loan agreements. So FRAs provide a good but inexact hedge against future borrowing costs. Borrowers wishing to use FRAs to hedge their risk should ensure that all their LIBOR-linked funding agreements use the derivatives market standard for LIBOR in their loan agreements – the British Bankers Association interest settlement rate.

Forward/forward loans and deposits

The predecessor of the FRA was known as the forward/forward loan and deposit contract and was developed in the 1970s. It was derived from a combination of, say, a six-month borrowing and a three-month deposit. Unlike an FRA, the forward/forward was not cash settled. It created an actual borrowing or a real deposit of three months in three months' time. Thus the bank was obliged to lend funds to a customer on the maturity of the forward/forward loan contract, and the price quoted included the lending margin for the particular customer.

Forward swaps

The term 'forward' confusingly is also used to denote forward swaps. These are not forward contracts, but foreign exchange contracts that alter the maturity date of a contract. They are also known as 'foreign exchange swaps' or 'forex swaps'. These are distinguished from forward outright contracts.

A forward outright is the classic forward contract entered into by a corporation to exchange currencies at an agreed rate in the future. A forward swap is a financial instrument banks deal in, but only the major corporate treasurers. The interbank market for foreign exchange consists mainly of spot dealing. When a customer requires a forward outright contract, the bank enters into the spot market as there is no forward outright interbank market. Say the customer wants to buy British pounds and sell US dollars in one year's time. The bank will buy the GBP spot versus USD. That leaves the bank with a time shift exposure. To eliminate this, the bank will enter into a forward swap which is a package of two legs – the bank will sell GBP spot versus USD, and simultaneously buy GBP versus USD forward for value one year. This reverses the spot contract and moves the GBP/USD position forward to match the customer's forward outright contract requirement.

Forward/forward swap

A variant on a forward swap is a forward/forward swap, which should not be confused with a forward/forward loan or deposit contract described above. The forward swap moves a foreign exchange position from spot to a date in the future. The forward/forward swap moves the position from one date in the future to another date in the future.

Futures

As stated previously, futures are forward contracts traded on an exchange. The contracts dealt by the recently-released-from-prison Nick Leeson, were futures contracts based on the Tokyo stockmarket. To a greater or lesser extent, all derivatives provide leverage. When an investor buys a government bond or a share he pays cash for it – upfront. Under an OTC forward contract, the treasurer has to satisfy the company's bank of its creditworthiness.

Under an exchange-traded futures contract, the investor has to place margin – initial and variation. Initial margin represents the exchange's view of what an investor could lose in a bad day. It is like a deposit against possible next-day losses. Recall that the Singapore futures exchange, SIMEX, doubled initial margin following Barings' difficulties. Variation margin reflects the actual movement in the market and has to be settled immediately. So unlike a forward contract, a futures contract has no built-up value at any time. The investor gains and loses on a day-by-day basis as con-

'. . . unlike a forward contract, a futures contract has no built-up value at any time.'

tracts are effectively marked to market. This makes futures the most transparent of derivative contracts. Funds have to be authorized and raised daily to cover losses. Losses cannot be carried forward on a year-by-year basis, as happened at Showa Shell of Japan.

Options

The price of an article is charged according to difference in location, time or risk to which one is exposed in carrying it from one place to another or in causing it to be carried. Neither purchase nor sale according to this principle is unjust.

ST THOMAS AQUINAS

An option gives the holder, on payment of an insurance premium, the right, but not the obligation, to buy or sell something in the future at a specified price and on a specified date or between specified dates. Nothing particularly new here. In the 1630s there was a market in Holland in tulip bulb options. At the height of this Tulipmania, the wife of a tulip option dealer thought that the tulip bulb brought home by her husband was an onion. She proceeded to cook it.

Listed options take the form of warrants. Options can be to buy one currency for another at an agreed exchange rate, the strike price. Options are also written on individual share prices or stock market indices such as the London's FTSE 100. An option to buy something is a call option, whilst an option to sell something is a put option.

Such options include the interest rate options sold without authority by the British local authority, Hammersmith & Fulham to generate cash and thereby bypass the UK government's external financing limit. As happened with Tulip options in Holland, the market crashed when demand disappeared. In the late 1980s a UK conglomerate in its take-over procedures for a UK utility company, bought options from its investment bank on a basket of other similar utility company stocks. But be careful here, as in certain jurisdictions such an operation could be deemed to be insider trading. S&P 500 and FTSE 100 options are used to provide guaranteed no-loss investment products.

Currency options

A currency option gives the holder, on the immediate payment of a premium, the right, but not the obligation, to buy a specified amount of currency A and sell a specified amount of currency B at a specified exchange rate and on a specified date or between specified dates. A European option gives the holder the right to exercise his option on only one date, the exercise date. An American option gives the holder the right to exercise the option at any time from the deal date to the exercise date. Exercise takes place two business days from the date of exercise in the case of currency options.

Asian options are quite different and are average rate options. At the end of the contract period, the strike rate is compared with the average rate observed for the currency exchange. If the strike rate is favourable to the holder of the Asian option, the option is exercised by way of cash settlement. Note that the average used can be observed daily, weekly, monthly or simply the difference between the start and end date of the contract. Asian options are useful for hedging currency exposure where management accounts are translated on an average rate for the accounting period and are misleadingly cheaper that American or European options. They simply cost less because of the statistical fact that an average of a price series is more stable than any particular price series. Asian options are cash settled automatically. Be careful about the basis for the averaging, as the bank providing the average rate option may be in a position to manipulate the fixings in its favour. A noisy operation in the foreign exchange market just before a fixing by a major foreign exchange

> *'It is much easier to eliminate doubts before dealing than after contracts are exchanged and positions hedged in the market.'*

bank can have a marked impact on the exchange rate for the few minutes it takes for the fixing to be made.

Atlantic or Icelandic options are similar to American options in that they can be exercised at any time between two dates, but the first date is not the deal date of the option, but some agreed date in the future, obviously before the maturity date.

In the financial markets everything is negotiable, all derivatives can be tailored to meet customer needs and exercise terms can be agreed between the parties. As with all financial instruments, it is vital to check details with your counterparty before dealing. In the case of currencies, a call option on an exchange rate can be confusing and care must be taken to avoid misunderstandings. The call could be a right to buy GBP and sell EUR or the call could be the right to buy EUR and sell GBP. So tell it like it is – ask for a GBP call, EUR put if that is what you want. If there is even the slightest doubt, specify the contract being discussed clearly. It is much easier to eliminate doubts before dealing than after contracts are exchanged and positions hedged in the market. Short cuts may sound highly professional but could lead to embarrassment.

Option-dated forward contracts

These contracts were available long before currency options and in fact used to be known as currency options. An option-dated forward contract is a forward exchange contract where the customer has the right to choose when to exchange currencies between two specified dates. This allows for delays in shipment or payment of underlying trade transactions. These are purely bank-to-customer contracts and generally are not available in the interbank market.

The choice of date feature in option-dated forwards is an interesting parallel with American currency options. Pricing is based on the worst rate for the option period. Consider the EUR/GBP currency pair. On 26 July 1999 the spot rate was EUR/GBP 0.6634. The six-month outright rate was 0.6720. So to buy EUR paying GBP, it would be better to pay 0.6634, the rate at the spot date rather than 0.6720, the rate at the six-month date. The worst rate for the period for a customer buying EUR on an option-dated basis would be 0.6720. Conversely, a customer buying GBP versus EUR on an option-dated basis would be quoted the worst rate of 0.6634, the spot rate. So if you are of a mind to buy EUR against GBP six months forward on an outright basis, ask if you can have an option-dated forward contract. You will probably still be quoted the same rate as the forward contract.

I did this regularly whilst in charge of currency management at an AAA corporation. It then occurred to me one night that this was a licence to print money. So I employed my strategy a few times, and the banks were happy to oblige. The strategy worked wonderfully, but my conscience got the better of me. There were some drawbacks to making myself a fortune out of it. Firstly, I could not do enough business in my own name to make it worthwhile. Secondly, my firm did not pay me performance-linked bonuses. Thirdly, the treasury of my firm was not a profit centre, so I could not just manufacture profitable deals. And finally, and fatally, I started feeling sorry for the counterparty banks! I could not employ the strategy later as a banker, because option-dated forward contracts are not available interbank, but I did advise my employers and clients not to enter into them with corporate clients.

If you can work out my strategy, send me an e-mail to we@dc3.co.uk

Interest rate guarantees (IRGs)

An interest rate guarantee is an option on a forward rate agreement. On payment of an option premium purchasers have the right, but not the obligation, to fix an interest rate for a specified future period in a specified currency for a specified notional principal amount. As with FRAs the interest rate fixing is on LIBOR. There are call IRGs to protect against upward movements in LIBOR and put IRGs to protect against downward movements in LIBOR. Under FRAs, a buyer wins if LIBOR rises and loses if LIBOR falls. However in a call IRG, whilst the buyer is compensated by the seller or writer if LIBOR rises, the buyer is under no obligation if LIBOR falls. For such insurance protection the buyer has paid a premium. Settlement is as with FRAs at the beginning of the interest period. Unlike currency options, there is no exercise to make as settlement is automatic.

Interest rate caps and floors

An interest rate cap can be thought of as a strip of call interest rate guarantees and an interest rate floor is a strip of put IRGs. So a cap is a strip of call options on FRAs. Automatic settlement takes place at every interest period on the same basis as with FRAs with one exception. Settlement takes place at the end of each interest period with no discounting.

Warrants

Warrants are essentially standardized options listed on a stock exchange in the form of capital market products. They can be options to buy or sell a particular bond or equity. They are also warrants on commodities such as gold, copper or oil or on particular currencies or equity indices. In the case of warrants on equities, the issuer of the warrants may not be issuer of the underlying equities.

Swaps

I've seen things in the market where I scratch my head and can't imagine why people did it. For example, when P&G lost all that money, I couldn't fathom what anyone at that company was thinking when they looked at that formula of the swap and said, 'Yes, that's exactly what I want to put on.'

ANONYMOUS AUTHOR,

'Confessions of a Structured Note Salesman',

Derivatives Strategy, 11 November 1995

Over time the term 'swap' has come to mean very different things. There are foreign exchange swaps also known as 'forex swaps' or 'F/X swaps'. As has already been mentioned, these swaps are also called forwards in the interbank market. The term 'swap' is now more commonly used for interest rate and currency swaps.

Interest rate swap

An interest rate swap is, in essence, a series of FRAs priced at a flat rate across all the legs of the constituent FRAs. These swaps allow a borrower to covert its medium- to long-term floating-rate liabilities to fixed-rate liabilities and *vice versa*. Such swaps allow savings banks to provide fixed-rate mortgages whilst raising funds in the floating-rate note market or through refinancing short-term money-market borrowings.

Interest rate swaps are more precisely known as 'single currency interest rate swaps'. They can be floating/floating, in the form of say, three-month LIBOR to six-month LIBOR or floating/fixed rate. The swap typically takes the form of one party paying a LIBOR-linked amount and receiving a fixed-rate amount applied to a notional principal amount for each interest period of the swap which would have several interest periods of three- or six-months amounting to several years. There will be net settlement of the interest-linked amounts. As with caps and floors, settlement takes place at the end of each interest period with no discounting. Legally these are contracts for differences, and the amounts paid are not regarded as interest. In general, interest rate swaps do not have to have net settlement. A 'annual vs 3s' swap would have one party paying a fixed rate annually in arrears and the other party paying three-month LIBOR. A 'semi vs 6s' swap would have net settlement, as the swap net settles amounts based on a fixed rate paid six-monthly and six-month LIBOR.

Currency swap

Currency swaps were originally simply a series of forward exchange outright contracts priced at a flat rate, and were distinct from forward exchange swaps which time-shifted currency exposure. Currency swaps were tailored to meet customer demands and in the days of exchange controls were done between two multinational corporations on behalf of their subsidiaries in each other's countries. BP, for example, could obtain US dollars for its US operations from Ford of the US and Ford UK could obtain sterling from BP's head office in the UK.

Currency swaps now take the form of cross-currency interest rate swaps. These are generalized single-currency interest rate swaps with the liabilities in different currencies. They can be floating in one currency exchanged for fixed in another currency or floating to fixed or even fixed to fixed.

A zero coupon fixed to zero coupon fixed cross-currency swap is essentially another form of an outright forward contract. The forward swap rates used by banks to generate outright forwards are based on interest rate differential between the two currencies. But in a forward contract, there is no explicit payment of interest. In this particular form of cross-currency interest rate swap the interest-related amounts are rolled up and settled simultaneously on maturity.

Swaptions

A swaption is an option on a swap and is crucially different from a cap or a floor. A cap is a *series* of options on short-term (typically three-month) interest rates, but a swap is but one option on a medium-term interest rate (say five years). Some of the component options in a cap may prove to be in-the-money and valuable, whilst others turn out to be out-of-the-money and valueless. A swaption is exercised once, if at all, during the option period. There are two forms of swaption, originally distinguished by the similar terms 'swaption' and 'swoption', though the latter name is uncommon now. A swaption can be an option within a certain option period to enter into a swap of certain period; or a swaption can give the right within the option period to enter into a swap maturing on an agreed date. The notional principal amount is specified under the contract.

Creating hybrids using building blocks

Due to my inexperience, I placed a great deal of reliance on the advice of market professionals . . . I wish I had more training in complex government securities.

ROBERT CITRON,
former treasurer, Orange County, California

Forward exchange contracts

The most basic hybrid financial instrument is none other that the forward exchange outright contract illustrated earlier. Forward exchange contracts to buy one currency versus another at some specified date in the future are not traded in the interbank market but are a hybrid product built from the interbank financial instrument building blocks.

A forward outright is the combination of a spot contract and forward exchange swap.

Break forwards

The break forward which is featured in Chapter 7 is another hybrid financial instrument. The break forward was a combination of a forward contract to buy currency A and sell currency B at a fixed forward rate and an attached optional contract, an option, to do the opposite, sell currency A and buy currency B, at a different rate, the break rate. In addition under the break forward, there is no premium paid upfront. The insurance costs are built into the prices of the two explicit contracts and these are settled on maturity. The construction of the break forward therefore requires another contract, a loan contract to defer the payment of the implicit option premium.

The three products together through the put–call parity principle of options actually result in being equivalent to another option: an option to buy currency A and sell currency B.

Asset swaps

An asset swap is a combination of an asset plus an interest rate or currency swap used to change the nature of the asset. These are sold as packages to banks seeking high-yielding floating rate assets. Bonds tend to be more volatile than loans which are infrequently revalued. When a bond, typically fixed rate, falls in price because of adverse news of a company, asset swappers buy them at a discount. They attach a fixed/floating rate interest rate swap to them, so that the package becomes a look-alike loan but with a higher than normal margin over LIBOR – essentially accounting innovation.

Conclusion

So recall that the key financial instruments referred to at the beginning of this chapter were: the spot contract, the forward contract, the option contract and the deposit contract. I have listed only a few hybrid contracts, but there is an infinite number of them. The message here is that if you understand the basic building blocks and that they can be combined with themselves or with each other in various ways, you not only understand all of the financial products that have been invented, but more importantly, most – dare I say all – of the financial products likely to be invented.

Don't focus on derivatives. One of the most dangerous activities of banking is lending.

ERNEST PATRIKIS,
Federal Reserve Bank of New York

CHAPTER 6

Derivatives for the retail client

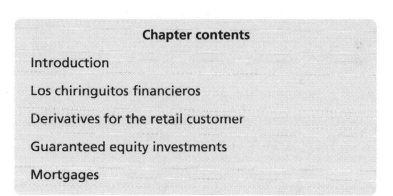

Chapter contents

Introduction

Los chiringuitos financieros

Derivatives for the retail customer

Guaranteed equity investments

Mortgages

Introduction

Should new financial instruments be sold to the retail client? Of course they should! Product development must be a customer-driven approach, and the financial markets must be tweaked to fulfil the needs of the retail client. One could say that all financial products have a retail client as an end-user. If an investment bank sells a swap or equity option to a savings bank, that savings bank could use it to structure mortgage or investment products for its clients who are retail clients. Stretching this principle, a foreign exchange transaction with a corporation such as an airline or travel company could help the retail customer-facing company to stabilize the prices of its holidays. But I believe that great care must be exercised in selling derivatives and other highly structured products *direct* to Joe Public. There is always the danger that the investor may claim, truthfully or otherwise, not to have understood the product and declare that it was mis-sold. Even selling structured products through intermediaries can be fraught with difficulty. Banks providing fixed-rate mortgages have had problems in demanding the replacement cost when such a mortgage is repaid early.

This chapter looks at some of the issues surrounding derivatives for the retail client with a few interesting and revealing stories.

Los chiringuitos financieros

Whilst writing this book in London, I received a telephone cold call. It was not the regular call from someone trying to sell medical insurance or office stationery. The saleswoman wanted to sell cigarettes in bulk. What intrigued me was that the telephone call was from Spain. I could hear Catalan being spoken in the background and the caller gave me a Barcelona telephone number.

> *'The main argument . . . against encouraging the private investor to enter the world of derivatives is one of investor protection'*

'A very special offer. Cigarettes normally costing 25 pounds for 15 pounds. A minimum of three cartons. All famous English and American brand names – Marlboro, Camel, etc.'

It seems that some of the shady financial operators or 'chiringuitos financieros' have moved on to cigarettes from the futures market! This chapter considers whether futures and options and other derivatives contracts are appropriate for the individual borrower or investor.

The main argument, and a very powerful one at that, against encouraging the private investor to enter the world of derivatives is one of investor protection – not only protection against fraud but also shelter against unsuitably risky investments.

In March 1994, futures fraud surfaced in Catalunya. Several cases illustrated how simply through telephone selling and the allure of untold riches more than 500 investors were relieved of up to 20 million pesetas each. Clients were selected through the business pages of the telephone directories. My sister-in-law, Matilde, was called at her hospital laboratory in Banyoles.

Matilde: '*I am not looking for any more investments.*'

Chiringuito financiero: '*Frankly, I am hardly surprised that you don't need any more investments. All the more reason for me to be interested in talking with you, madam. It is clear to me that you keep yourself well-informed. I would just like to inform you of our product which may be of interest to you.*'

The brochure of the company based in Zug, Switzerland, included a photograph of cows grazing in a lush mountain valley. The Tokyo Stock Exchange trading floor featured on the cover, whilst inside were pictures of an oil refinery and glistening gold bars. The text, whilst emphasizing the firm's expert capabilities, did not understate the possibility of loss.

'*As is explained, stockmarket speculation is accompanied by significant risk. In the case of options and futures, it is possible to lose one's entire capital. The price analysis and speculation of the highly expert and specialized fund managers are not guaranteed. The markets are subject to a multitude of external influences, in part, unpredictable.*'

The risks of market loss were thus well-outlined. However, those that took the bait were not exposed to market risk – the funds were never ever invested in the futures and options markets, but diverted to Aruba in the Netherlands Antilles! Emphasizing the dangers merely served to indicate concern, customer care and professionalism. The silent implication given was '*Are you "macho" enough for this investment?*'

Derivatives for the retail customer

Retail derivatives have been used for the protection of the individual investor or borrower against a variety of risks.

Derivatives could allow house buyers to lock into the level of house prices whilst saving for a down-payment. Property or real estate futures were developed by the London Futures and Options

Exchange, but for a variety of reasons did not succeed. Real estate futures have recently been launched in Chicago.

Borrowers can also protect themselves against rises in mortgage interest costs. Savings banks enter into fixed-floating interest rate swaps or swaptions and offer fixed-rate loans to clients.

Exchange rate protection could be available prior to a family holiday in the US. In the late 1980s, Barclays Bank offered low principal currency options through its branches.

All praiseworthy concerns, but the derivatives market is, in general, quite unsuitable for direct use by non-high-net-worth individuals. Most derivatives are, by nature, standardized. Individuals, however, have non-standard needs and risks. Any mismatch (basis risk) may well exceed the client's risk.

Derivatives do, however, have an increasing place in retail banking and insurance. Fixed-rate and maximum rate mortgages can be provided by banks and savings institutions, with the financial institution covering its interest rate exposure to a subsequent rise in interest rates through the derivatives market. The client does not deal with derivatives, but is provided with a seamless package. He gets what he wants – a fixed-rate mortgage – and the bank manages the risk for itself in the wholesale futures and swaps market. Savings products with 'embedded' derivatives are now commonplace. Zero-coupon deposit structures have been offered to the retail market. The interest rate risk for the savings bank is covered through structured zero coupon swaps.

A more recent innovation takes the form of stockmarket index-linked deposits or bonds offered by banks. The bank provides a deposit investment with the value rising in line with the growth in the Ibex35, the Spanish stockmarket index with a guaranteed return of capital invested. But there is no interest on the deposit. The effective interest-free deposit allows the bank to protect itself by purchasing or constructing an option on the Ibex35. I recommended such an investment (with a prime Spanish bank) to my sister-in-law in Banyoles. However, I was astonished at the bank's approach of only answering broad questions and only on the telephone. Given the undoubted standing of the institution concerned, a brochure providing full details of the investment in print was surprisingly not forthcoming. If highly structured transactions are sold cheaply over the telephone, then financial institutions must ensure that its telephone operating staff are adequately trained to cope with searching questions. Perhaps a contradiction. Perhaps the internet could prove ideal in that the bank selling the product could even provide a several thousand word explanation of its products at negligible cost. No staff training would be required, as customers would be expected to read the literature and understand the product themselves. Questions could be answered not by low paid

> *'...financial institutions should make use of the variety of options, futures and swaps available to satisfy their customers' investment and financing requirements.'*

and hardly trained telephone-sales staff, but via e-mail which would allow a considered answer then to be posted up on a 'Frequently Asked Questions' page ready for the next potential customer.

In conclusion, raw derivatives should not be actively marketed to individuals. However, financial institutions should make use of the variety of options, futures and swaps available to satisfy their customers' investment and financing requirements. It is incumbent on these institutions, however, to ensure that their customers have absolutely no doubt as to what they are entering into and the risks inherent – including in the case of fixed-rate mortgages, any early repayment penalties or with respect to investments, premature encashment terms.

Guaranteed equity investments

Since the late 1980s, guaranteed investment schemes have become commonplace from the UK to Ireland to Spain and South Africa. They all rely on derivatives to provide the downside protection promised, and they tend to be treated as deposits or insurance policies rather than equity unit trusts.

The earliest and therefore simplest of such guaranteed schemes were as follows: A principal sum was invested with a bank and a guaranteed return was provided at the end of five or seven years. 'Double-your-money' schemes were popular at a time of high interest rates. To provide a 100 per cent return in five years, a compound annual rate (CAR) of 14.9 per cent is required. To double investments in seven years, only 10.4 per cent is needed. The principal guarantee under these guaranteed investments was structured through zero coupon interest rate swaps. Often the return was exaggerated through the quoting of simple interest in bold large type in advertisements – 20 per cent per annum in the five-year case – with the CAR in much smaller type.

The major variation on such pure deposit structures was the introduction of equity index linking. Now just the return of principal investment was guaranteed. The investment return was linked to the return on one stockmarket index such as the FTSE 100. Neither interest nor dividends were paid. The term was typically five years.

Again zero coupon interest rate swaps provided the guarantee, and so as to provide the equity linking, equity index options were purchased.

The investment would be treated in the UK either as a bank deposit or as a single premium insurance policy. Therefore the return being the difference between the deposit and the final maturity value was taxed either as interest or in accordance with the taxation on insurance policies. In most such cases there was no actual equity investment by the retail investor, so capital gains treatment did not apply – i.e., there was no capital-gains-tax-free allowance.

There have been many variations under the basic structure depending on the current level of interest rates and market volatility, and therefore the pricing of the zero coupon swap and the equity option.

The guarantee was sometimes reduced to less than the principal invested, say 90 per cent of the principal amount to provide more for the equity option. Sometimes there was a guaranteed minimum maturity value of greater than the initial principal invested, say 110 per cent of principal. This reduced the amount available to the bank to purchase equity options.

Under the rationale of providing smoothing of equity markets, instead of providing a return based on the growth over five years, the final fixing is now usually the average level of the index over the final year. This effectively reduces the term by half a year. This smoothing operation has been taken further. Not only is the final year's equity index averaged, but so also is the first year's index.

Later, the equity linking was spread to more than one country's stockmarket index. Nationwide Building Society's 'World Guaranteed Equity Bond' provided an investment linked to the average performance of six world markets with a return of capital guaranteed if left for six years. The return was calculated on the difference between the average of the first year and the average of the final sixth year. Maximum returns are linked to twice the investment or 12.25 per cent CAR. All this averaging serves to dampen returns. An investor would be far better off with six separate guaranteed equity bonds guaranteeing return of capital, but providing benefits in line with market growth in the individual markets.

Barclays Bank's subsidiary, B2, markets a product providing linking to equity returns through a monthly savings scheme whilst guaranteeing the return of capital invested.

Mortgages

In March 1999, Nationwide, the UK's largest building society, launched a euro-rate mortgage in the UK. In itself this was nothing new, as a number of UK banks including Barclays and Abbey National had already offered such mortgages soon after the introduction of the euro. But what was different was that, while being linked to the interest rate environment in Europe, the European Tracker Mortgage operated entirely in sterling. As far as the borrower was concerned, there would be no exchange rate risk on the interest payments or on the repayment of principal.

Nationwide's chief executive, Brian Davis said: 'For those who are keen to link their mortgage to European interest rates, it is the first mortgage available in the UK to provide that opportunity with all payments required in sterling.' To me, this mortgage is a curious hybrid, as it appears to serve the needs of interest-rate speculators rather than hedgers. It is not a natural hedge for those with euro income or assets, nor is it a natural liability for purely UK-based borrowers. But it serves those who wish to benefit from lower current euro interest rates. Given the higher margin over market rates, it is a bet on sterling remaining outside the euro and having higher interest rates.

The Nationwide product involved a ten-year variable rate mortgage, with rates set at 1.75 per cent above the European Central Bank (ECB) base rate, with a discount of 1 per cent in the first year. During the first ten years, the interest rate will continue to be set at 1.75 per cent above ECB base rate, and will reflect changes. At the end of the ten-year period, the rate will revert to Nationwide's standard variable rate. This compared with true euro mortgage rates of 1.5 per cent above EURIBOR.

'So how did the Nationwide hedge its bets?'

The pricing of the mortgage includes very stiff redemption fees. Early redemption fees will be payable if all or part of the mortgage is repaid, or transferred to another product, during the first ten years, as follows: years 1 to 5: nine months' gross interest; years 6 to 8: six months' gross interest; years 9 and 10: three months' gross interest.

In a falling interest rate environment, the ECB rate should lag EURIBOR, and in a stable environment, the ECB rate should be about 0.25 per cent above EURIBOR.

So how did the Nationwide hedge its bets? It did not run the exchange rate risk as reported in the press, but involved the Nationwide buying a Quanto swaption, i.e., it bought a two-month option to enter into a ten-year interest rate swap to pay three-month EURIBOR and receive sterling three-month LIBOR. Both interest-related amounts are determined using a sterling principal. What is worth noting in such a swap is that the natural day basis is different between the two currencies. Sterling is quoted on a 365-day basis whilst EURIBOR is quoted on a 360-day basis. This makes a small difference of 7 basis points at interest rates of 5 per cent or so, but will be significantly higher if such a structure was applied to currencies with higher interest rates. At rates of 15 per cent seen in the UK a decade ago, the difference would be 21 basis points.

How was the Quanto hedged by the bank providing the hedge? Probably by finding someone on the other side. Quantos were first seen linked to dual-currency notes, where the interest was linked to one currency's benchmark, but denominated and indeed payable in another currency.

Perhaps the Nationwide could have cut out the middleman investment bank by creating its own deposit structure with interest rates linked to the ECB? Or issue a Quanto bond or note structure to appeal to investors.

And finally . . .

The key to successfully managed financial instruments is to create structured asset or liability instruments. But then instead of going into the market to hedge such structures, savings banks should engineer liability or asset structures that have equal and opposite properties.

III

Studies in innovation:
from creativity to closing

The examples of innovation in this part go through the thinking process behind two of the financial products I developed in the 1980s, the break forward and perpetual swap. The entire financial product innovation process is walked through from conception to creativity to communication and closing. Both cases refer to products that were initially tailormade solutions to actual customer problems. The solutions were then turned into products for customers with similar problems. Both were also partly driven by the inconsistent taxation treatment of financial products. A lesson to be drawn is the need to maintain customer dialogue. The secret of financial product innovation is not high technical ability to price and manage complicated financial derivatives. The key financial instruments are those that reflect customer needs, are simple to put together and can be explained in 30-second sound-bite. There are very few genuine new financial products. Many products developed more than a decade ago are now finding themselves being re-invented. The product featured in the first case study, the break forward was re-invented in 1998. Amazingly this was done by the very same bank that originally created it.

The break forward

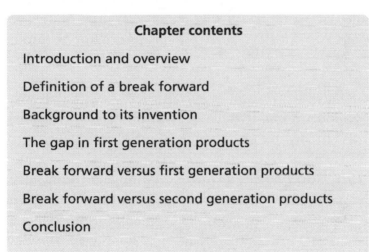

Introduction and overview

The case studies in this and the following chapter walk through the thinking process behind two of the financial products I developed in the 1980s. The first of the two case studies on the break forward relates to events in 1986 when currency and other options were only just being introduced into Europe. The term 'derivative' had not yet been coined. Legal documentation was very much done on a case-by-case basis. There was no ISDA and no British Bankers Association deal terms for derivatives. Legal documentation for swaps, for example, often took more than a year to process. In short, we were in the frontier stage for derivatives.

The break forward came about not as a result of a product looking for a client, but very much the other way around. We had a problem in that these new-fangled options were not selling despite their insurance-like benefits. Customers did not want to pay upfront options premiums. So we were selling deep out-of-the-money options as a way of minimizing option premiums. But such out-of-the-money options were close in function to no hedge at all.

'What was the essential property of the contract? It was a hedge with holes.'

Customers had, by then, got used to forward exchange contracts, and the standard procedure was to fully cover everything in the forward market. But to produce an option that was close to a forward contract would have meant a very high option premium. We are back to the problem of nobody wanting to write out a cheque for option premiums. So we had to construct a package of a forward contract plus an option to unwind the forward contract. And the premium? The option to unwind would probably be out-of-the-money, so it would be small. Nevertheless, we could bundle it into the price of the forward contract. Hey presto! The premium disappears and what we have is just a contract that looked like and largely behaved like a boring old-fashioned forward contract but with a twist.

And there was also a problem with the taxation treatment of these options. It took a good few years for the Inland Revenue to understand these new instruments and produce a fair and neutral tax treatment. Option premiums were not always tax deductible, I discovered at my regular lunch with my colleague in the taxation department. He suggested that I find a way to bundle the option premium into the price of the contract. I broke into an extremely wide grin. *'I've just done that, Brian.'* Not only would the break forward be more appetizing to the treasurer but also to his tax accountant.

At that time there were a number of option strategies going by names such as 'collar' and 'cylinder'. What was the essential property of the contract? It was a hedge with holes. One evening, draining away freshly cooked pasta, I thought, 'Aha! I'll call this product a colander'. A hedge with the ability for the hedge to be released! But no, I did not name the product a colander. It was not meant to be a flashy new turbo-charged product. I designed the break forward to be a boring and slightly but significantly different variation on an old favourite that the client's board of directors had become familiar with. It was a forward contract with a break. I therefore named it the 'break forward'.

Definition of a break forward

A break forward contract is a forward contract at a forward rate that permits the holder to break or unwind the contract with an opposite transaction at another rate, the break rate.

There is no option premium payable and the costs of the embedded option are included in the fixing of the forward rate and the break rate.

Background to its invention

I created the break forward at Midland Bank with the help of Edmond Levy, to solve two problems – firstly, the reluctance by finance directors of corporate clients to pay premiums and secondly, an unsatisfactory tax treatment.

In October 1986 currency options had only recently been introduced to the UK. Companies were still very reluctant to pay option premiums in advance. Under standard forward exchange contracts, no premiums were payable. The client simply entered into a contract with a bank for the exchange of, say, US dollars for GB pounds for delivery in six months' time. At maturity, the two currencies were exchanged at the pre-agreed exchange rate and for the amounts specified. And by 1986, the exchange commission that had been commonplace a decade earlier had all but disappeared. So companies were not asked to make any payment upfront when they entered into forward contracts and they were going to take a lot of persuading to write a cheque in payment for a currency option. Some treasurers did persuade their boards to allow them to enter into options. However, many found that if the options, which were after all a form of insurance against adverse currency movements, were not exercised at maturity, they were criticized with the benefit of hindsight by their boards. '*We needn't have bought those new-fangled options,*' they were told. '*Let's stick with forward contracts.*' So a structure was required with option characteristics but with no explicit premium for the customer to pay.

At that time, I happened to have lunch with my colleague, Midland's taxation manager Brian Atkinson. Apparently, in addition to the corporate treasurer's reluctance to pay premiums, there was a significant tax problem. If the option was not exercised, the premium paid would not be tax deductible and turn out to be a wasting asset. There would be no tax loss generated to offset against profits. The treatment was therefore asymmetric and therefore highly unsatisfactory. However, the UK inland revenue was comfortable with forward contracts, and if we could structure an option to look like a forward contract, then all would be well.

As it happens, I was also puzzled as to why when options were sold, they were persuaded to buy out-of-the-money options, rather than in-the-money or at-the-money options. A deeply out-of-the-money option has the properties of no contract at all, whilst a deeply in-the-money contract was almost certainly going to be exercised. Corporates traditionally covered everything in the forward market, so for me the first step into the options market should be something that behaved more or less like a forward contract and not like something that was no hedge at all. So my first brainwave was to sell deep in-the-money European type options – new slim-line DIET options! Of course they did not get off the ground for hedging purposes, because deep-in-the-money options cost a lot more than out-of-the-money options, and corporates were reluctant to pay large upfront premiums. So I had to think of another structure. But before we consign DIET options to the derivatives graveyard, they turned out to have quite a useful property as an off-balance-sheet deposit and loan structure. Because of the large premium payable, the pricing was simply based on the forward exchange rate and the interest rate. The moral here is never discard a solution just because it does not work. It may work splendidly for a completely different purpose. Disasters are indeed opportunities.

So the break forward contract was constructed as a synthetic currency option. This chapter explains that the implied and embedded premium is the difference, in money terms, between the fixed rate, which coin-

> *'The moral here is never discard a solution just because it does not work. It may work splendidly for a completely different purpose.'*

cides with the strike rate of the synthetic option, *inclusive of the premium*, and the break rate, which corresponds to this strike rate.

In managing foreign exchange exposure, the traditional hedges employed are forward exchange contracts or those arising from appropriate transactions in the spot exchange rate and related money markets. We might denote such hedging instruments as first generation products. The experience of high exchange rate volatility and the accepted rigidity of forward contracts created the need for more sophisticated and flexible exposure management instruments. Currency option contracts marked the beginning of the second generation. Such contracts were distinguished from conventional forward contracts in that the purchaser of a currency option is merely obliged to deliver an upfront premium to ensure protection against downside currency risk.

Break forwards were a new product developed by Midland Bank which combined the best features of both generations. Break forward contracts provide corporate treasurers with a hedging instrument which can mimic both fully forward hedged and unhedged strategies as well as the continuum of positions in between these extremes. Furthermore, the product was designed to overcome the corporate treasurer's aversion to upfront premiums and their associated taxation difficulties. There were circumstances where option premiums paid did not secure tax relief; given that break forwards do not involve the payment of a premium, this difficulty did not arise. This chapter identifies and clarifies the bridge that break forwards provided; in addition it carries out a comparative cost analysis of break forwards relative to other hedging instruments.

The gap in first-generation products

The example I focus attention on is that of a UK corporate treasurer seeking to manage the exposure generated by a US dollar principal sum which he anticipates having to pay in three months' time. Of course the principles and analysis applied here are not specific to this case and can be extended to other situations in a similar manner.

I shall be working with a particular representation of such cases and so it is best if, by way of introduction, the familiar scenarios are considered first.

A treasurer of a UK importer of US goods expecting to pay dollars in three months' time may by using 'first-generation products' choose either to leave his position exposed to fluctuations in exchange rates or to hedge his position by buying today in the forward market at (say) GBP/USD1.5000. For completeness, assume a current spot exchange rate of GBP/USD1.5130 with volatility at 14.60 per cent. These parameters are not crucial to the discussion other than providing a possible indicator of the future spot rate in relation to the forward exchange rate. The outcome from these two decisions is presented in Figure 7.1.

The horizontal axis denotes the spot rate on maturity of the forward contract whilst the vertical axis denotes the exchange rate at which the treasurer effectively exchanges currencies under the alternative strategies.

The forward deal ensures that the treasurer receives USD1 for every GBP0.6667 irrespective of the spot rate outcome on maturity; hence the forward position can be represented by the line HH'. On the other hand the unhedged position, represented by UU', enables him to take full advantage of favourable spot movements; but he leaves himself exposed to unlimited downside risk.

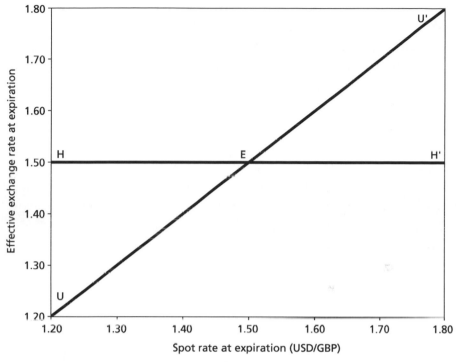

Fig. 7.1 ● Effective exchange rate at expiration

Currency exposure relates to the effects currency movements
have on the cash flows and financial structure of the firm. A major
concern for the treasurer is to adopt hedging strategies that minimize the danger of incurring a serious risk of loss should exchange
rates move against him. Few people would disagree that the decisions taken by treasurers in the management of exposure need to be
monitored and continually assessed, but there is some doubt surrounding the criterion by which such decisions are judged.
Generally, exposure management performance is measured relative to some exchange rate yardstick. This yardstick is, however,
often chosen retrospectively as the optimum exchange rate available
over the exposure period; that is, the most favourable amongst the
various forward rates that become available from the time the exposure is identified and the subsequent spot rate that arises on the
maturity date of the transaction. In such cases the treasurer's efforts

will inevitably attract criticism, as the evaluation would always be made with the benefit of hindsight.

Ideally, the treasurer would like a hedging instrument which ensures that he has the best of both positions; that is, one that enables him to exchange currencies at the ruling spot rate, should it be greater than 1.5000, and at GBP/USD1.5000 should spot fall below 1.5000 – effectively he would like to ensure the line HEU'. The case illustrated here relates to the exposure management of a UK importer. The ideal effective rate for a UK exporter would be that represented by the kinked line UEH'. This would constitute a hedged position with rates above 1.5000 and an unhedged state below that rate (ignoring bid–offer spreads). This requires the ability to make dealing decisions with hindsight knowledge of the spot exchange rate outcome. Such a product is, of course, unobtainable in the marketplace, but through break forwards the treasurer can come close to it.

Break forward versus first-generation products

Behind a break forward contract is the explicit acceptance by the treasurer of a fixed rate, at which he is obliged to purchase dollars, set worse than the ruling forward rate. The selling bank values this disadvantage and provides the treasurer with an option to unwind the 'fixed' position at a predetermined strike price, the 'break rate'. The break-facility under a break forward contract is the following right: having bought dollars at the fixed rate, the treasurer can sell back the dollars at the break rate. He is then free to buy his dollars again in the market, but at the ruling spot rate. Clearly this can only be to his advantage if, on maturity, dollars can be purchased at a more favourable rate than the break rate, i.e., when spot is above the break rate. (Of course he is also free to take advantage of favourable forward rates should they occur at any time throughout the life of the contract, knowing that the fixed obligation can be unwound at no worse a rate than the break rate.) Figure 7.2 presents three such break forward contracts.

The first break forward contract, S, assumes a relatively small

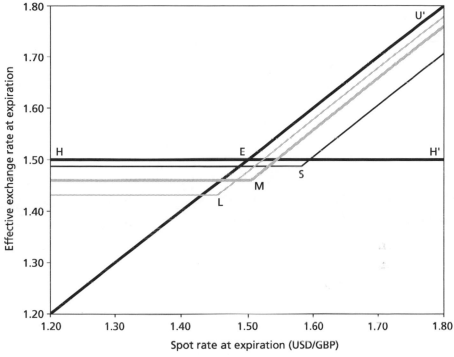

Fig. 7.2 ● Effective exchange rate for various contracts at expiration

loading (1.00 per cent) on the forward rate, yielding a fixed rate of 1.4850. Under our market assumptions, this enables the treasurer to break at 1.5825. With the forward rate at 1.5000, this three-month European option to break the fixed obligation is out-of-the-money. As one might expect, the higher this loading, the 'better' will be the break rate in that, for a given movement in spot, it is more likely that the break-facility will be activated. Thus we might choose to define a medium loading as one where the break rate is at-the-money (in relation to the forward rate) and a large loading as one which ensures an in-the-money break-facility. With our assumed market conditions, an at-the-money break rate will be obtained with a loading of 2.90 per cent (i.e., a fixed rate of 1.4565). The third contract in the diagram above assumes a relatively large loading of 4.80 per cent (fixed rate of 1.4280) yielding a break rate of 1.4505. The effective exchange rates at which currencies are exchanged under each of these contracts is represented by the lines S, M and L. The kink in these lines represents the point beyond which the treasurer is able to take advantage of favourable spot rates by activating the break facility. Note that Figure 7.2 is also applicable to a particular forward rate available at any time during the life of the contract for the same value date.

At one extreme we can regard a conventional forward exchange contract as a break forward with a zero loading; one providing no option to unwind. Likewise, the unhedged position can now be given the representation of a break forward contract with an infinite loading; one where the fixed position is certain to be unwound to take advantage of favourable spot rates (thus the fixed rate would be equal to the break rate). Hence it only remains for our treasurer to specify a loading which best reflects his views on how much downside risk he is willing to accept.

'For any chosen loading, the break forward provides a backstop should the outcome of spot on maturity be widely at variance with the treasurer's expectations.'

This choice of loading should depend on three factors:

- his capacity and willingness to accept risk;
- his views, if any, on the likely direction or trend in spot movements and the degree of certainty with which such beliefs are held; and
- his accounting treatment and performance measurement, i.e., is he judged against:

    1. the forward rate at the time the exposure is identified; or
    2. the spot rate on maturity of the foreign currency exposure?

For any chosen loading, the break forward provides a backstop should the outcome of spot on maturity be widely at variance with the treasurer's expectations.

We will show that if the choice of hedging instrument is restricted to either a forward exchange contract or dealing spot for the same value date, the opportunity loss, that is, performance measured relative to the optimum, can be unlimited should the wrong instrument be used. However with a break forward contract, this loss is always limited.

Exposure management evaluation

Consider first the case where the treasurer is judged relative to a forward contract. Here a highly risk-averse treasurer would aim at a minimal loading so as to eliminate all downside risk and effectively lock into the forward rate *irrespective of his views on spot movements*. Such a treasurer is blind to opportunity loss in that he is willing to forgo all potential benefits to be earned should spot move favourably relative to the forward rate. Break forward contracts are aimed at those who are aware of such an opportunity and wish to insure against its loss. A loading on the forward rate is precisely the premium due for insurance against this opportunity loss. As in the case with general insurance policies these premiums can be reduced, but only if the insured is willing to forgo some of the compensation he would be entitled to (e.g. accepting a GBP100 excess on a motor car policy). The larger this excess (i.e., the distance between the break rate and the traditional forward rate), the smaller the loading.

Figure 7.3 is constructed by measuring break forward contracts relative to the fully forward covered position. That is, S_1, M_1 and L_1 are the vertical distances in sterling terms between HH' and S, M and L, respectively, in Figure 7.2. It is apparent that, for a given loading, break forward contracts offer considerable advantages over the forward contract whilst still retaining downside protection against exchange rate risk. Note how, under these contracts, the benefits are obtained earlier the larger the loading on the forward exchange rate highlighting the premium/excess trade-off.

When performance is measured relative to the subsequent spot rate (e.g., when establishing accounting profits or losses), the highly risk-averse treasurer would adopt a fully unhedged position irrespective of his views on spot rate movements. Note that the analysis

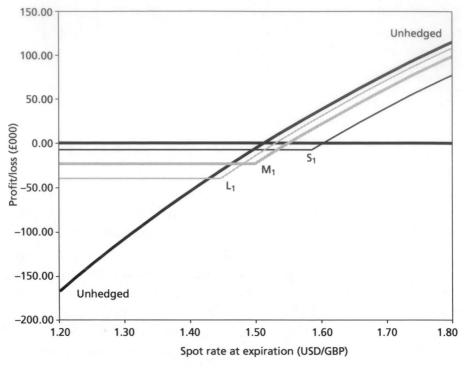

Fig. 7.3 ● Break forwards measured relative to forwards

here applies equally well to performance measured relative to a forward rate that becomes available for the same value date. Here, the prime concern becomes the opportunity loss relative to the forward exchange contract should the spot rate move unfavourably. If such movements occurred, then the unhedged strategy could lead to a harmful economic exposure on the business. For example, the firm's competitors could have covered themselves in the forward market and guaranteed a price in sterling terms. Our treasurer, however, would be forced to either charge his UK customers an exchange surcharge and incur adverse market sentiment or else suffer losses. Again, break forward contracts can be viewed as providing insurance against such losses. In this instance, however, the premium is the money value of the difference between the fixed and break rates, with the excess being the loading on the forward rate.

Figure 7.4 is constructed in a similar manner to that of Figure

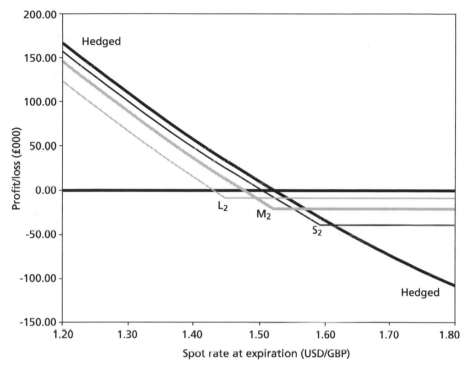

Fig. 7.4 ● Break forwards measured relative to spot

7.3, but now break forward contracts are measured relative to the fully exposed position. The lines S_2, M_2 and L_2 are the vertical distances, in sterling, between S, M, L and UU' of Figure 7.2.

Choice of break forward loading

The treasurer's choice of break forward loading is not only dependent on his view on spot rate movements and on how firmly such beliefs are held, but also on his willingness or authority to bear risk. These factors should combine to produce an optimal break forward loading which could in theory be any figure between zero and infinity. The extremes are, as we have already seen, the conventional forward hedge or a fully exposed position. Such positions are rarely the best strategies for the majority of situations.

I have argued that for highly risk-averse treasurers, there is no desire to do any better than the criteria by which they are measured. That is, deal forward if performance is measured relative to the forward rate, or leave the position exposed and deal at whatever spot rate occurs on the value date if performance is measured relative to that exchange rate. At the other extreme we have the risk lover with a view, however flimsy, that spot (or a subsequent forward rate) will be one side or other of the ruling forward rate. Such a treasurer will put all his eggs in one basket and either leave his funds exposed or will fully forward cover his funds.

Both such types of treasurers could suffer under one or other performance criterion should they be applied subsequent to the outcome of the spot rate on the value date (as depicted in Figure 7.1). Consider however one who takes out a break forward contract. Recall that for our example the ideal position is represented in Figure 7.2 by the kinked line HEU'. The line M, representing the medium loading break forward, remains roughly equidistant from HEU'. That is, whatever the spot rate is on the value date (or any subsequent forward rate for the same value date), the treasurer does no worse than exchanging at about 2.90 per cent the wrong side of the optimum rate.

Treasurers typically do not hold identical views on spot movements, nor do they perceive risk in a like manner. Thus a medium-loading break forward will not be suitable to all situations. Those whose performances are measured relative to the forward rate and perceive risk according to that measurement will be tempted towards a smaller-loading break forward contract, such as that depicted by S or in extreme circumstances a forward contract. Likewise, those whose performances are measured relative to the spot rate on the value date and perceive risk according to that criterion might well prefer a larger loading break forward contract such as that represented by L.

An equally important factor is the treasurer's view of how spot will move through the period of the contract. This could either strengthen his demands for a small or large loading or could act as an opposing force. For instance a moderately risk-averse treasurer (I will term him a risk manager), who perceives risk as the loss relative to forward cover, may think it quite likely that spot will move favourably relative to the forward rate. In such instances he would prefer a contract which offers flexibility, so that should the outcome of spot coincide with his beliefs, he is able to exchange at the more favourable rate. Thus, although a forward contract or low loading break forward contract might initially be desirable, his views would lead him to accepting a medium break forward loading, the extent of this increment being largely determined by how firmly such beliefs are held and how much risk he is willing to bear.

The number of such examples one could invent are too many to consider here in any detail. It is useful, however, to summarize suitable loadings under various scenarios in the form of charts (see Figures 7.5 and 7.6) dependent on the choice of performance criterion. These can be used as ready-reckoners in choosing a break forward loading. The axes measure the probability, in the treasurer's view, that the spot rate will move favourably relative to the ruling forward rate and his degree of risk-bearing capacity. These, together with his chosen performance criterion, will indicate the appropriate break forward loading. Whilst such constructions are largely subjective containing many 'grey areas', sensible finetuning will be applied by the user as necessary.

Break forward versus second-generation products

The evaluation of break forward contracts measured relative to spot, in Figures 7.4 and 7.6, brings out an important interpretation of such contracts as currency options.

One of the basic results from option-pricing theory is that the combination of a dollar put/sterling call option with a forward purchase of dollars versus sterling is simply an option to call dollars/put sterling. The break-facility component of our break forward contracts could be

'It should not be surprising . . . to find that break forward contracts are equivalent to pure option contracts . . .'

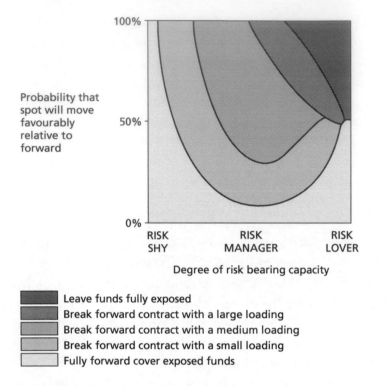

Probability that spot will move favourably relative to forward

100%

50%

0%

RISK SHY

RISK MANAGER

RISK LOVER

Degree of risk bearing capacity

■ Leave funds fully exposed
■ Break forward contract with a large loading
■ Break forward contract with a medium loading
□ Break forward contract with a small loading
□ Fully forward cover exposed funds

Fig. 7.5 ● Choice of contract for treasurers who measure their performance relative to forward

viewed as the free provision of European dollar put options. As with all options, their value, if any, will depend in part on the intrinsic value of the option – in this case, the difference between the strike price and the ruling forward rate. It should not be surprising therefore, to find that break forward contracts are equivalent to pure option contracts, since the former entail a forward commitment coupled with a reversing option.

Suppose that, rather than take out break forward contracts, our treasurer were to purchase dollar call options with strike rates at 1.5825, 1.5000 and 1.4505. The premiums for these options, compounded over three months, are the maximum loss relative to spot under their respective call option. Under a corresponding break forward (when the break rate is set at the call option strike rate), the maximum loss relative to spot is equal to the difference between the fixed rate and the break rate in money terms. At the

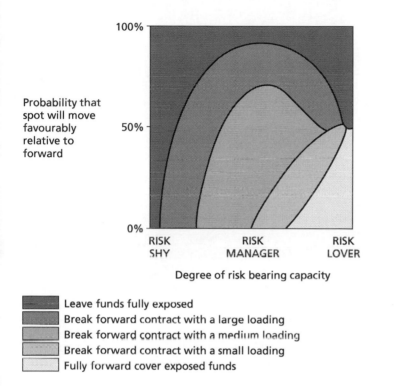

Probability that spot will move favourably relative to forward

100%

50%

0%

RISK
SHY

RISK
MANAGER

RISK
LOVER

Degree of risk bearing capacity

Leave funds fully exposed
Break forward contract with a large loading
Break forward contract with a medium loading
Break forward contract with a small loading
Fully forward cover exposed funds

Fig. 7.6 ● Choice of contract for treasurers who measure their performance relative to spot

extremes, we can see that an infinitely large difference between the fixed and break rates (resulting from a zero loading or a forward contract) would be equivalent to an option with an infinite premium (i.e., a deep in-the-money option). On the other hand, a break forward with the fixed rate equal to the break rate (resulting from an infinitely large loading) would be such that the corporate would suffer no loss versus spot and must therefore be equivalent to an option with a nil premium (i.e., a deep out-of-the-money option, or a fully exposed position).

In general, then, the following rule applies: small-, medium- and large-loading break forwards for the purchase (sale) of dollars are equivalent to purchases of, respectively, in-the-money, at-the-money and out-of-the-money European dollar call (put) options. In every instance the fixed rate in a break forward contract (representing the worst rate the treasurer receives) is precisely the strike

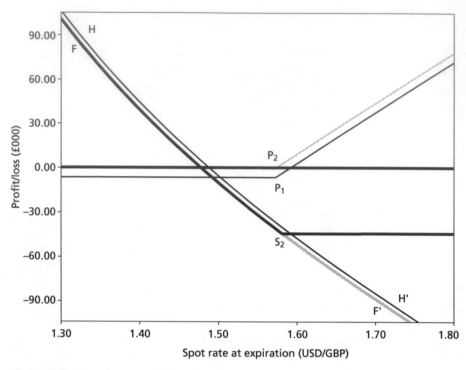

Fig. 7.7 ● Constructing a synthetic call option

rate under the corresponding option, but with the premium (suitably compounded) incorporated into that rate.

This recognition of break forwards as synthetic options can be seen diagramatically. Suppose a do-it-yourself small-loading break forward contract is constructed by combining an out-of-the-money put option (represented by P_1 in Figure 7.7) with a forward purchase. The overall position is given by the sum of the vertical distances of the lines P and HH′ measured from the zero axis at each spot rate. This results in the line S_2.

As can be seen the premium paid for the put option has been converted via the forward contract into a call option. However, whereas the put option is out-of-the-money, the call option is in-the-money, and hence its associated premium is larger.

It is important to notice that this synthetic call option entails the payment of a premium as required by the put option. Break forward contracts however do *not* require any such payment. The insight by which such contracts can be offered is made immediately obvious once it is seen that S_2 can be constructed in an infinite number of different ways. One in particular is to move P_1 upwards until the horizontal segment coincides with the zero axis (thus eliminating the premium) and then to compensate this movement by shifting HH' across to the left accordingly. These two movements give rise to P_2 and FF'. The line P_2 represents a free put option with a strike rate at 1.5825. This option is paid for indirectly through the commitment of a forward purchase of dollars at a fixed rate set worse than the forward rate, i.e., at 1.4850.

It can be seen that the break forward contract can be used whenever options are thought desirable by choosing the break rate to be equal to the desired strike price. In the UK in the mid-1980s customers liable to capital gains tax treatment on currency forward and option contracts recognized that the break forward contract had a major advantage

'Break forward contracts were uniquely valuable tools for managing foreign exchange exposure and with their potentially fiscally efficient properties marked the beginning of third-generation treasury instruments.'

over over-the-counter options. Unlike a currency option, the break forward contract did not entail payment of an initial premium which, in the case of an option, could have become a wasting asset affording no tax relief. Break forwards thus economically dominated currency options in that they were tax-efficient instruments.

Option contracts are flexible instruments for coping with natural option-type exposures. Setting aside any view the treasurer may have on spot rate movements, recall the basic rules for deciding when to use option contracts rather than forward contracts.

'Whenever a quantity of foreign currency receivable (payable) is uncertain, buy a put (call) option on the currency. If such sums are known, then a forward contract is appropriate.'

These rules apply equally well to break forwards, i.e., such receivables (payables) can be hedged by selling (buying) the currency forward using a break forward contract.

Conclusion

The break forward transaction involved the sale by the bank to a customer of foreign currency at a particular rate. However this rate is subject to the right of the customer to sell back a currency at a lower rate if he wishes. Accordingly the Inland Revenue treated them as two separate transactions with tax treatment in line with the traditional treatment of foreign exchange forward and spot contracts. The Revenue saw no option premium. Break forwards also met the needs of finance directors who did not want to be seen to be paying an option premium. They never had to justify the payment of an upfront fee for foreign exchange forwards. So the products clearly met a need, and moreover the bank supplying them was seen to be making an effort. That effort was rewarded not only in sales of break forwards but also in sales of standard products.

Break forward contracts were uniquely valuable tools for managing foreign exchange exposure and with their potentially fiscally efficient properties marked the beginning of third-generation treasury instruments. We have seen that the structure of such contracts is flexible enough to imitate both traditional forward and option contracts as well as the unhedged position.

Perhaps a fairer and more suitable measurement of a treasurer's performance is obtainable with the introduction of second- and third-generation foreign exchange products. Currency options limit downside risk whilst providing scope for taking advantage of favourable rates of exchange over the period of the exposure. It is often remarked that performance should be measured relative to some yardstick which is adjusted in some way to reflect the degree of volatility the market experiences. Break forward contracts can provide an adjusted forward rate (the fixed rate) which reflects the market's valuation of a treasurer's views and risk characteristic. Until a better yardstick is found, the success of a treasurer's exposure management efforts is best measured relative to this optimal break forward contract. These contracts combine discipline with motivation and a good defence against critics.

The pricing and quotation of break forward contracts can be carried out to suit the customer's preferred position. Midland Bank quoted such contracts given either the break rate or the preferred loading on the forward exchange rate.

And finally . . .

Just two weeks after Midland Bank launched the break forward, Hambros Bank announced the FOX – a forward contract with an optional exit. Nevertheless, this was no 'me-too' copy cat product. It had taken us several months to develop the break forward including pricing systems, legal documentation, back office processing and risk management, and I am sure that it would have taken Hambros just as long. Moreover, they could just as well have launched two weeks before us. It just goes to show that however wonderful your product is, somebody else can launch it just before you.

What happened next? Well, pretty soon, I applied the break forward concept to forward rate agreements and interest rate swaps. I reconstructed interest rate guarantees or options on FRAs, creating break FRAs also known as 'limit FRAs'. The immediate next step was to repackage interest rate caps into break swaps, also known as 'limit swaps'.

About six months after the launch of the break forward, Salomon Brothers launched the participating forward. This could have been called a 'part break forward'. Instead of having the right to unwind the entire forward contract, the customer could unwind only a portion of the contract. However, for this benefit on only a part of the forward contract, the customer could start benefiting at the forward contract rate itself instead of at the break rate. He could 'participate in the upside benefits'.

Economically, a generalized participating forward could have been created simply through any desired customer-chosen combination of a normal forward exchange contract and a break forward.

CHAPTER

8

Perpetual swaps

Overview

This second case study describes a product developed in 1988. Again the product was not developed in a vacuum, but in response to repeated requests by clients for a solution to a problem.

The hedging of transaction exposure was described in the case study on the break forward in the previous chapter. The problem solved through the creation of the perpetual currency swap was that of translation currency exposure. Both such exposures are fully described in Appendix 3, 'Risk management terms'.

A number of company boards at that time increasingly felt that translation exposure should be managed by them. The traditional method for managing such translation exposure was for companies to borrow in local currencies. Through such borrowing, natural hedging will occur. This case study describes the creation of a currency swap that was arguably more efficient than foreign currency borrowing – the perpetual currency swap – and illustrates the benefits of examining not just the pre-tax but the post-tax effect of managing translation exposures. Such an off-balance-sheet hedge can help to minimize balance sheet size and provide a more cost-effective solution.

Introduction

Essentially, transaction exposure covers the valuation in a firm's home currency of foreign currency receivable or payment. It concerns the valuation of real transactions. It deals with cash flow. Translation exposure, on the other hand, deals with a stock concept. It is the sensitivity of the value of a foreign-currency-denominated asset or liability to changes in the value of that foreign currency with respect to a firm's home currency. A UK firm with a large US subsidiary is required to revalue the US subsidiary in sterling terms on its annual balance sheet date. Even if the US subsidiary is highly profitable, a significant fall in the US dollar with respect to the GB pound would lead to a translation loss for the UK company.

> *'Essentially, transaction exposure covers the valuation in a firm's home currency of foreign currency receivable or payment.'*

I do not intend to discuss the pros and cons of translation exposure management in detail as there is still quite a difference of opinion. This chapter assumes that hedging the sterling value of a capital investment was regarded as a 'good thing'. It therefore walks through the background to the development of a novel, elegant, efficient and effective structure for hedging such translation exposures – the perpetual currency swap.

We at Charterhouse Bank had been discussing such translation exposures for some time without any solution. By way of general tax education, a seminar was arranged at a major accountancy firm. It turned out to be quite a tedious presentation, not helped by the poor air-conditioning on a hot summer's day. The speaker droned on and on outlining the tax treatment of various derivative products – the term 'derivative' had by then arrived in the UK. I was just about to fall asleep when something he said jolted me out of my slumber. I began to doodle furiously. I had come up with a solution to our problem.

I find attending seminars extremely valuable but not for what I can learn at the seminars. Information can be gleaned from many a textbook or downloaded from the internet. What I find really valuable, even listening to a lifeless monotonously read-out speech, is my lack of concentration. So often something the speaker says can spark an idea perhaps in quite a different field. Very often the most effective financial products are cross-markets products. A commonplace application or widely understood process in one market can be tweaked to provide a revolutionary product in a different market. 'Think everywhere,' I wrote in Chapter 2, 'How to capture the big new IDEA'. I do my best thinking at seminars.

Where?

To my knowledge, the 'perpetual' or 'capital-hedging swap' first appeared in the autumn of 1988 independently out of Midland Bank and Charterhouse Bank. Structures with some similarities were also produced by S. G. Warburg and Citibank. The swap was soon widely available from other banks through dissemination by corporate clients to their relationship banks in search of a better price and also through the movement of bank staff to other banks (see Chapter 13, 'Dangers and disasters; profits and principles'). The swap structure has been variously known as the 'capital-hedging swap', the 'perpetual currency swap', the 'revolving currency swap', the 'callable currency swap', the 'cancellable currency swap', the 'evergreen swap' and the 'extendible swap'.

What?

Essentially the perpetual swap was a cross-currency cross-callable floating/floating interest rate swap with an undetermined maturity date. As with plain vanilla currency swaps there may or may not have been an exchange of principals at the beginning.

The floating/floating payments were typically linked to 12-month LIBOR, so as to cover an annual accounting date. At the end of each LIBOR period, both parties had the right to call or cancel the swap.

Economically, the swap replicated hedging through a rolled forward series of forward exchange contracts. Like a rolled foreign exchange contract, there was no cash settlement at the end of each leg. But unlike a rolled forex contract, which would have fallen foul of Bank of England regulations against transactions at off-market rates, the swap was not rolled; it was simply not terminated until either party opted to do so. Moreover the cross-option to determine the maturity date provided conditionality to the swap and deferred the disposal date for tax purposes.

There was a variable margin payable or receivable on one of the LIBORs. This reflected the bank's costs of capital, any mismatch between the forex market and the LIBOR pair, the funding cost or benefit of any position built up through the bank swapping forward in the market and, of course, the bank's financial engineering profit.

Illustration of a perpetual swap

For an illustration of the perpetual swap for a United Kingdom plc investor with a subsidiary in the United States, see Figure 8.1.

Start date: time (0)

UK plc effects a sterling rights issue to buy a US company for USD100 million. As the first leg of the perpetual swap, it purchases the USD100 million out of sterling at spot (–2) from the bank counterparty where spot (–2) was the GBP/USD spot exchange rate quoted at time (–2) for delivery at time (0).

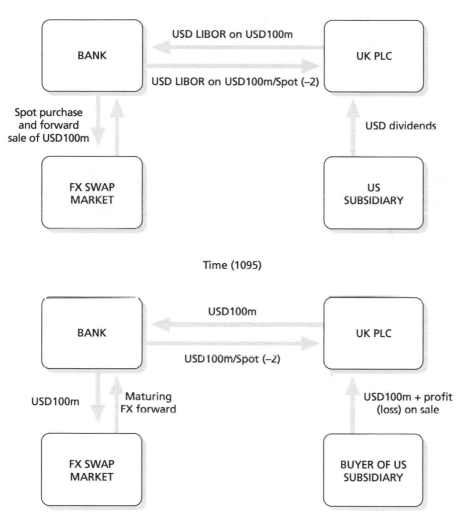

Fig. 8.1 ● Perpetual on capital-hedging swap

UK plc commits to pay at time (365) an amount equivalent to the 12-month USD LIBOR fixed at time (−2) on the USD100 million.

In addition, UK plc agrees to receive at time(365) an amount equivalent to the 12-month GBP LIBOR, also fixed at time (−2), less a margin, on the sterling amount of GBP100/spot (−2). The variable margin, quoted by the bank and agreed by UK plc, may be positive or negative depending on the forex forward market.

UK plc agrees to sell USD100 million for sterling at spot (–2) to be exchanged at some future interest related payment date. When either party exercises its option to determine the exchange date, the swap terminates.

Time (363)

At time (363), both parties have the right to effect the termination of the swap as at time (365). The bank quotes, if it so chooses, a margin above or below its payment of sterling LIBOR for the following year for value time (730). If acceptable, both parties agree for UK plc to pay 12-month USD LIBOR on the USD100 million and receive 12-month GBP LIBOR, less the positive or negative margin on the original sterling amount at time (730).

Time (365)

If there is no agreement the transaction terminates as at time (365), with the USD100 million exchanged for sterling at spot (–2). The LIBOR-linked amounts determined at time (–2) are exchanged.

Time (728), time (730)

The processes at time (363) and time (365) are repeated, with either party having the option of terminating the swap at time (730). Under mutual agreement, the swap continues for another year.

Time (1093)

At the end of three years, say, the parties agree to terminate the swap as at time (1095).

Time (1095)

The swap terminates.

UK plc sells USD100 million for sterling at the exchange rate spot (–2). Delivery risk mitigation clauses could include settlement on a net basis against the spot exchange rate fixed at time (1093).

Termination reasons

There are several possible reasons for the termination of the swap. Reasons include: disagreement between UK plc and the bank on the margin; full utilization of the bank's credit line; absence of a novation clause; UK plc's disposal of the underlying asset; and UK plc's capital gains tax (capital gains tax) management.

Margin disagreement

UK plc is uncomfortable about the size of the sterling LIBOR margin and has not succeeded in renegotiating it.

Given that both parties have the right to terminate the swap, there is no value in having a fixed margin, below sterling LIBOR. With a fixed margin, the swap would result in being in one party's favour at the roll-over date. The termination provisions would be activated.

The variable margin quoted by the bank and the bank's right to terminate can be seen as major disadvantages to the structure. The savings generated through the use of the competitive one-year forex market and the credit line and capital efficiency of the product should more than compensate. The corporate treasurer, however, should place himself in a position to calculate and argue for a fair margin.

Credit considerations

Exchange rates have substantially moved, with the US dollar appreciating against sterling. Whilst the value of UK plc's US real asset has appreciated, a credit position will have been built up against it and in favour of the bank under the swap.

This would be reflected initially in an increased margin deducted from sterling LIBOR. Eventually the exposure might result in becoming a 'large exposure' in the central bank's eyes with respect to a transaction with a small bank. A credit line greater than 10 per cent of a bank's capital base is uncomfortably large, whilst over 25 per cent is impossibly large.

'There are several possible reasons for the termination of the swap.'

A termination by the bank for credit reasons should not give rise to a major problem for UK plc. A capital gains tax loss would be generated which could be used within UK plc against capital gains tax gains or carried forward within the company. Note that, whilst a funding requirement might result in a cash outflow, under a longer-term swap the bank would have assumed the worst possible outcome over the period and calculated the credit line accordingly. There is no point paying for a credit line unless it is needed. Material adverse change clauses can be quite useful to banks.

No novation clause

There is no novation agreement within the swap. The structure through leakage by corporate customers and staff moving from bank to bank soon became common knowledge. With the novelty of the structure gone, the bank should be prepared to novate all or part of the perpetual swap to another bank with an appetite for the credit risk. This would avoid a cash flow or tax event for UK plc under current tax legislation.

Hedged investment disposal

Termination could occur as a result of UK plc's requirements. The US subsidiary could have been disposed of. The currency gain or loss under the real asset would need to be offset by a loss or gain under the swap.

In general, however, the swap would be terminated at the same time as the real asset was sold and not at the annual payment date. A provision to terminate the swap within a roll-over period should be included in the terms of the perpetual swap.

Tax management

UK plc wishes to generate a capital gains tax gain or loss under the perpetual swap as part of its tax management. It could create a capital gains tax gain to offset capital gains tax losses incurred in the current year or carried forward from previous years within UK plc. A capital gains tax loss generated to offset other capital gains tax gains within UK plc would also free up bank lines.

A new perpetual swap would be effected simultaneously to maintain the hedge.

Why?

There were a number of advantages to this translation exposure management structure. These include:

- the control of the corporate's balance sheet size;
- the tax treatment of the perpetual swap as compared with that of other hedges;
- good liquidity and therefore availability;
- fine pricing;
- capital efficiency and bank credit line efficiency.

Disadvantages were the bank's right to terminate and the variability of the margin quoted by it.

Balance sheet reduction

The standard method of hedging translation exposure is to use foreign currency borrowing.

But why borrow if there is no need for external funds? The perpetual or any off-balance-sheet hedge eliminates the need for funding in the currency of investment. It allows the use of funds held on deposit in sterling or a sterling rights issue. If financing is indeed needed, it can be sourced through the medium and currency which most highly rates UK plc and therefore provides it with the lowest price.

'The standard method of hedging translation exposure is to use foreign currency borrowing.'

Increased borrowing solely for hedging purposes might also impact on gearing covenants.

Taxation

Under the then UK tax system, long since changed, exchange differences on capital borrowing were generally not recognized for tax purposes. The disposal of the capital asset, i.e., the US subsidiary, and the sale of the dollar proceeds at spot fell under capital gains tax. There would not, therefore, be matching for tax purposes by an exchange loss under a capital borrowing.

Forward disposals of foreign currency through forward contracts or currency swaps also came under the scope of capital gains tax.

Hedging through forward contracts, however, represented unconditional disposals of the foreign currency as at their *inception* dates for capital gains tax purposes. A sale of dollars under a long-term currency swap would also represent an unconditional capital gains tax disposal as at its inception date (unless a suitable conditionality clause was installed). This would not only result in a timing mismatch, but also the books would have to be kept open for some years with possible tax penalties.

The perpetual swap represented a conditional contract. Remember both parties had the right to terminate. The date of disposal of the currency was not known at the outset. The perpetual currency swap incorporated a cross-option whereby either party can determine *when* the currencies are to be exchanged. For capital gains tax purposes, therefore, the disposal of currency takes place when the currencies are exchanged unconditionally; i.e., on the termination date.

Liquidity/Availability

The swap should be made available in most currency pairs. The swap is derived from the foreign exchange swap market. In fact, the perpetual is hedged by the bank through a series of forwards. So long as a forex forward exists in the currencies, the perpetual swap can be structured.

Unlike the cross-currency interest rate swap market, the forex forward swap market is liquid even in minor currencies (subject to exchange controls).

The hedge will have to be terminated in the event of the asset disposal. Long-term forward contracts or currency swaps are difficult to unwind. A forward contract is, effectively, a cross-currency, zero coupon fixed/fixed interest rate swap. Volatility of interest rate differentials would result in a loss or gain on disposal under such a hedge. On the other hand, the perpetual swap, which is a floating/floating swap, is relatively stable in the same way as a floating rate note is stable.

Pricing

Pricing of a product derived from the forex market should be competitive. By contrast, the medium- to long-term currency swap market is expensive. Unwinding costs are minimized under the perpetual.

Under the example, UK plc should have a good idea of a reasonable margin by obtaining quotes from the foreign exchange forward market. Given that the cross-currency LIBORs do not exactly derive the forex forwards, the margin will vary.

Capital efficiency

By maintaining the ability to terminate the swap within a year, the bank was able to regard the swap as a one-year transaction.

Under central bank rules, currency forwards and swaps required a capital backing of the mark-to-market value plus 1 per cent for transactions of up to one year of outstanding term or plus 5 per cent for outstanding terms of over one year.

This therefore led mechanically to a lower price relative to long-term swaps. This was simply on the basis of regulatory requirements – regulatory arbitrage.

Credit line efficiency

Credit considerations are similar to but not identical to capital constraints.

A bank credit-analyzing a five-year currency swap would look at the worst (95 per cent) case over the period and require a credit line of 40 per cent to 50 per cent of the notional principal amount. A one-year horizon would have required a line of 10 per cent to 20 per cent. Credit lines would be utilized only if rates actually moved, rather than by looking at worst case scenarios.

When?

The UK taxation rules changed soon. In March 1991 the UK Inland Revenue proposals provided for the recognition as income of exchange differences on all monetary assets and liabilities as they accrued on a translation basis.

Capital borrowing would no longer be treated as a 'nothing' but would get income treatment. Swaps and forwards would also be treated as monetary items and therefore any gain or loss on unwinding would be treated as income rather than suffer capital gains tax. There would be no provision to match a hedge to the underlying asset or liability. Furthermore, the income treatment would apply on a translation basis; i.e., marked to market every year.

Hedging a capital asset, such as a US subsidiary through the use of forex forwards swaps or borrowing would amount to a capital asset being hedged by a 'monetary liability' and generate a tax mismatch.

The Revenue wrote that:

> All monetary assets and liabilities whose treatment would be affected by the new scheme would be valued on the day the scheme came into operation. Any exchange differences arising subsequently would be calculated for tax purposes by reference to that valuation.

'Capital borrowing would no longer be treated as a "nothing" but would get income treatment.'

Existing perpetual swaps, unlike true long-term arrangements, could have been terminated on the introduction of revised taxation rules.

Conclusion

The perpetual, capital-hedging, callable, revolving or cancellable swap was a typical financial instrument engineered to overcome the perceived inconsistencies of the tax system. But tax management is a moving target. No sooner has a solution to a problem been created but the problem disappears or is transformed into quite a different one. Financial engineers soon structured products in line with the Inland Revenue's new rules. Nevertheless, whereas the modern marketing manager claims not to sell products but provide tailormade solutions, the perpetual currency swap product which lost its original rationale soon found other uses. Its efficient pricing mechanism remained. It was an ideal and efficient product for the currency hedging of investment funds.

And finally . . .

This second case study on the perpetual currency swap also illustrates tax benefits. In no sense would I regard myself as a tax authority. But in highly competitive markets and inconsistent tax treatments, focusing on solving taxation problems rather than fractions of a basis point was a far better return on time and effort invested. This product also featured regulatory arbitrage in that pricing was determined by the arbitrariness of capital adequacy rules which rose significantly on deals structured with maturities greater than one year.

Another lesson from the perpetual is the lack of proprietary rights over the structure. Now, however, at the turn of the millennium, business processes can be patented.

Finally, the perpetual currency swap's development illustrates, just as the creation of the break forward shows, the tangible benefits in cross-disciplinary teams, whether formal or virtual. These products were developed a decade before knowledge management became fashionable in management consulting.

From reading the press recently, you could be forgiven for thinking that risk management is a new issue.

JUAN PUJADAS,
Price Waterhouse

Risk management

The 1990s have seen a number of cases of spectacular derivatives losses. But what about the GBP15 billion losses sustained by the UK pensions industry for failing to use derivatives or derivatives techniques? These pensions providers casually provided minimum annuity rate guarantees in the late 1980s but neither managed nor re-insured the interest risk. By far the largest losses sustained by banks continue to be through plain old-fashioned lending. Nevertheless, derivatives pose a problem in that whilst profits can be made quickly so also can losses mount up.

Part IV, Risk management, includes hedge choice and performance measurement, a substantial chapter on legal risk management by Iona Levine, who set up and heads the derivatives legal practice at Hammond Suddards, and a chapter on the taxation aspects of derivatives and risk management.

There are no fundamentally new or different risks in derivative products, rather . . . familiar kinds of risks are presented and combined in novel ways.

―――――――――――――――――――

BRIAN QUINN,
director, Bank of England

Hedge choice and performance measurement

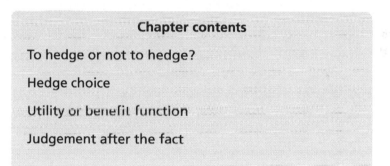

Chapter contents

To hedge or not to hedge?

Hedge choice

Utility or benefit function

Judgement after the fact

To hedge or not to hedge?

Boards have been for some time apprehensive about derivatives, following the losses sustained by firms such as NatWest bank on badly priced interest rate caps, Barings bank on Nikkei futures, Procter & Gamble on structured geared swaps, Orange County on structured geared bonds, Showa Shell on rolled over foreign exchange contracts, and Metallgesellschaft on long-term oil transactions managed with short-term oil futures. Some of the cases mentioned were not the fault of classical derivatives contracts at all. In one particular case it was credibly argued that the losses arose not because of the original derivatives contracts, but because of the unwinding of the contracts.

On the other hand, the successful case by the shareholders of a grain co-operative in the US against its board directors for *failing to hedge* exposures suggests that avoiding derivatives is not a safe option. Ignominious ignorance isn't blameless bliss.

A US Court of Appeal has ruled that 'directors breached their duty in failing to supervise (the) manager and become aware of essentials of hedging to be able to monitor business . . . the primary cause of the gross loss was the *failure* to hedge.' Without wishing to pore over troubled oil firms, nor water down the implications for treasury management, Corporate and Bank Boards of Directors and Central Bankers are rightly concerned about their firms' exposure to risk management instruments. The court case, however, suggests that throwing the baby out with the bath-water can be equally dangerous.

The US legal journal, *North Eastern Reporter*, related the ruling on 1 June 1992 by the Courts of Appeal of Indiana on the case of *Brane v Roth*. The case did not involve another 'blue chip' corporate or investment bank. It related to the activities of a small rural grain co-operative and shareholders' action against its directors for losses the co-op suffered in 1980 as a result of the directors' failure to protect its position adequately. The firm could have hedged in the Chicago Board of Trade grain futures market.

Nearly 90 per cent of the co-op's business was buying and selling grain. The directors met monthly reviewing the report of the manager who handled the grain transactions and the financial reports produced by the co-op's book-keeper. Profits had fallen in successive years since 1977 and after a substantial loss in 1979 the firm's accountant recommended that the directors hedge the co-op's grain position to protect itself against future losses. The directors did in fact authorize the manager to hedge, but despite grain sales totalling USD7,300,000, only USD20,050 in futures contracts were effected. The fall in the grain price resulted in a gross loss for the co-operative business in 1980 of USD424,039.

What could send shivers down many a directorial spine is the court thinking behind its finding that the co-op's directors breached their duty of care. They breached their duties by retaining a manager inexperienced in hedging; failure to maintain reasonable supervision over him; and failing to attain knowledge of the basic fundamentals of hedging to be able to direct the hedging activities and supervise the manager properly; and that their gross inattention and failure to protect the grain profits caused the resultant loss. The directors argued that they relied upon their manager and should be insulated from liability, the court ruled that 'the business judgement rule' protects directors from liability only if their decisions were informed ones.

As derivatives have become commonplace, the Indiana case does not appear to have been used as a precedent. But the publicity surrounding derivatives losses which might have tempted boards of directors to adopt the ostrich-like approach of leaving everything uncovered and blaming losses on the Bundesbank or the Japanese, Korean, Russian, Latin American financial markets could well rebound.

The BIS and central bankers regularly express

> *'The directors argued that they relied upon their manager and should be insulated from liability, the court ruled that "the business judgement rule" protects directors from liability only if their decisions were informed ones.'*

their fears over the burgeoning market in derivatives. Boards have in the past blamed unforeseen 'adverse exchange rate movements' at their AGMs to explain away their losses.

But equal attention must be paid to the management of 'natural' exposures generated by on-balance-sheet assets or liabilities. Will, for example, the non-executive directors of a savings bank be comfortable in allowing their treasurers to offer a supply of fixed-rate mortgages *without* a swap to hedge interest rate exposure?

On 10 April 1999, the *Financial Times* reported that 'Assurers may face GBP14 billion bill for pension guarantees'. The loss could have been mitigated through using derivatives.

The problem arose in the late 1980s when most pension funds in the UK wrote pension policies guaranteeing minimum annuity rates. A combination of falls in interest rates and lower mortality rates has made these guarantees valuable to policyholders.

It has been suggested that the problem arose from the 'fall in long-term interest rates'. It is true that rates did fall substantially and unexpectedly. But the problem for the insurance companies arose because of their collective failure to manage the risks inherent in the interest rate insurance policies sold to annuity policyholders. They should have taken out interest rate insurance.

There has been much discussion as to who should bear the strain – policyholders or shareholders. But insurance company management should face up to the responsibility for failing to use derivatives techniques, explicitly or implicitly, to manage the interest rate risk. The mismanagement of derivatives on a considerably smaller scale has led to jail, dismissals or resignations at Barings, NatWest, UBS, Hammersmith & Fulham and elsewhere.

The fall in interest rates has led to substantial gains in the gilt portfolios of life companies. Is the UK Treasury entitled to reduce its rates on long-term government bonds it has issued because rates have fallen? Of course not. It is two decades since futures and options arrived in the UK.

Even if derivatives are not explicitly used, ignorance of risk management techniques is no longer an excuse for failing to use them. And most of the major banking losses have not occurred through derivatives at all but through plain old-fashioned ill-judged lending. When I set up the new products development desk at a UK bank in 1984, my first task was to get the legal documentation and risk management under control for the then new products such as options, swaps and FRAs. But the documentation for forward exchange contracts was but a few lines. Why the inconsistent fuss for instruments that generated much lower risk? And there was no special risk management policy even for long-term fixed rate loans which could be regarded as floating rate loans plus fixed/floating swaps. Many UK government bonds had for many years dual dates. They matured at any time between two dates. And most floating rate notes had embedded minimum interest rates. No special derivatives policy was required for such instruments.

Hedge choice

The focus here is to introduce a way for a finance director and his treasurer to select a hedge given the nature of their institution's appetite for risk, its performance measurement yardstick and its forecasts on rate direction.

Should the option be out-of-the-money (OTM)? An OTM US dollar call option purchased by a corporation is such that it gives the buyer the right but not the obligation to buy US dollars against sterling at lower than the current forward rate – fewer dollars per pound. Should the option be at-the-money (ATM)? An ATM US dollar call option is to buy dollars at a rate exactly equal to the current forward rate. Would an in-the-money (ITM) option be advisable? An ITM dollar call is such that the rate is better (higher) than the ruling forward rate and consequently results in a higher insurance premium. *In extremis* an option to buy dollars at GBP/USD2.50 for a year would be a very deep ITM option. It would be almost certainly exercised. Therefore an extremely deep ITM option is an exact substitute for a forward contract which is bound to be exercised. An extremely deep OTM option is a substitute for an uncovered position or no hedge at all.

'The continued publicity surrounding billion dollar losses on derivatives suggests that a firm's appetite for risk is an important determinant of hedge choice.'

The continued publicity surrounding billion dollar losses on derivatives suggests that a firm's appetite for risk is an important determinant of hedge choice. There is, however, disagreement on how such decisions should be judged. 'Cover everything automatically in the forward market,' or 'Leave everything uncovered until spot and blame losses on the Bundesbank,' may be politically sensible approaches. Conventionally, option salesmen have advised corporate treasurers to buy OTM options. Why not ITM structures? Do they really cost more? Is a forward contract cost-free?

Premium bonds

I find the UK's premium bonds fascinating in terms of learning about investor psychology. Premium savings bonds, far from a new financial instrument, are a UK government security offered to individual persons and issued by the Treasury through the National Savings Agency. The details below have been obtained from the National Savings website: http://www.nationalsavings.co.uk

This retail savings financial instrument pays no interest. In lieu of interest, the GBP1 nominal bonds are included in monthly draws for cash prizes. These prizes are free of all UK income tax and capital gains tax. There is a prize fund for each month which is equal to one month's interest on each bond eligible for the prize draw for that month. The rate of interest used to create the prize money pool was 5 per cent in August 1998 (3.25 per cent per annum in June 1999). The rate of interest is changed from time to time to broadly reflect market interest rates.

As Christopher Moxey, National Savings' commercial director, commented: *'The tax-free Premium Bond prize fund rate equates to a return of 5.42 per cent gross at the higher rate of tax and just over 4 per cent at the lower rate. And, of course, no other investment offers its customers security of capital and the opportunity to become an instant tax-free millionaire.'*

In respect of each prize draw, there is one prize for every 19,000 bond units eligible for inclusion in that draw. Prizes range from one GBP1 million prize down to GBP50 prizes. Any surplus is carried forward to the following month's draw. A bond will be included in all draws in and from the second month after the month you buy it. The maximum holding per individual is GBP20,000.

So are premium bonds a good buy? Professor Terence O'Donnell wrote to *The Times* (Letters, 29 August 1998) suggesting that 'a wealth warning is needed on premium bonds publicity'. A maximum bond-holder of GBP20,000 would expect to earn 5 per cent or GBP1,000 in any one year of monthly draws. Professor O'Donnell based his warning on the fact that some 94,200 of 140,000 maximum bond-holders will receive less than GBP1,000, whilst about 40,000 will get more than GBP1,000. He calculated that GBP700 or 3.5 per cent is the most frequent size of annual winnings. I beg to disagree. I would suggest that premium bonds are an excellent buy even ignoring the tax benefits.

Herein lies the essence of risk and reward. Unlike bets with the UK National Lottery or any other gamble, capital, other than through the ravages of inflation, is preserved. Interest of GBP1,000 for a GBP20,000 bond-holder is forgone for the chance to win prizes of up to GBP1 million. In the UK National Lottery, only half of the ticket income is used to fund prizes. So to approximate to a maximum premium bond investor, someone betting GBP10 twice a week for 50 weeks on a lottery would expect a return of *minus* 50 per cent or winnings of GBP500 per annum. And there is no shortage of 'investors'. Lottery players dream of becoming millionaires and are prepared to forgo limited ticket purchase money. And investors/gamblers are quite rational. That is because for a limited loss and an almost unlimited gain they are prepared to accept poor expected returns.

As is discussed in Appendix 4, 'Islamic financial products', such lottery bonds are also used by Islamic banks to provide value in lieu of interest, and the UK bank Alliance & Leicester entered accounts opened in June and July 1999 into a weekly prize draw to double their money. But beware of imitating such structures, as lotteries are regulated in most countries, and in the UK National Savings has a monopoly.

In a casino's roulette table a zero and often a double zero are acceptable to gamblers. A player can walk away from the game (usually!) with, at most, the funds brought to the table lost. He puts up limited capital. The casino has an unlimited capital exposure and cannot, other than through bankruptcy, turn clients away. In the old television game 'Double Your Money' contestants often, quite rationally, took the money and stopped playing the game – even if on a simplistic probability calculation they should have continued. The value of the certain gain in-hand outweighed the possible benefit through a chance win of a larger sum.

Utility or benefit function

What was God's Utility Function? If there is only one Creator who made the tiger and the lamb, the cheetah and the gazelle, what is He playing at? Is He a sadist who enjoys blood sports? Is He trying to avoid over-population in the mammals of Africa? Is He manoeuvring to maximize David Attenborough's television ratings? These are all intelligible utility functions that might have turned out to be true. In fact, of course, they are all completely wrong. . . . The true Utility Function of life, that which is being maximized in the natural world, is DNA survival.'

RICHARD DAWKINS,

River Out of Eden: A Darwinian View of Life, Basic Books, 1996

A utility function, which could also be described as a benefit function, is a technical term used by economists. It defines what is being optimized or maximized. What is the point of the exercise? Utility theory concerns itself with defining value. How valuable are different outcomes to a decision maker? A utility function mathematically expresses and assigns a value to all possible outcomes. In portfolio theory the utility function expresses the preferences of economic entities with respect to perceived risk and return. What is the utility function of the coach of Barcelona Football Club? Bobby Robson, as coach of Barcelona in 1997 won the European Cup Winners Cup as well as two domestic Spanish cups. He was still fired! Why? Real Madrid won the Spanish league title that year. But his successor, Louis van Gaal, did win the league (and therefore finished ahead of rival Real Madrid), but was still vilified for not using enough Catalans.

'A firm's benefit or utility function should be developed based on risk appetite and its performance yardstick.'

Just as in the case of individual investors in premium bonds or gamblers in lotteries and casinos, corporations do not have linear relationships between profit and loss and benefit to the firm.

A firm's benefit or utility function should be developed based on risk appetite and its performance yardstick. Monetary profits and losses should be mapped on to benefit gains and pains. Perhaps the benefit function should be such that the pain value of a loss of USD200 million should be three times the pain value of a loss of USD100 million. Moreover, the benefit function will generally not be symmetric around a nil profit/loss result. The loss of USD200 million is generally much more painful for an organization than the positive benefit of a gain of USD200 million. The value of income is seldom disposable. It is with this very much in mind that a potential corporate buyer should examine the benefits of options sold by banks or the value of the services and claims of the various 'dynamic hedging' exposure management firms. These firms attempt to replicate options for their clients by putting on and then adjusting forward exchange contracts. Under this dynamic hedging system the client is not, however, comforted with the strictly limited exposure generated by an option purchased.

Judgement after the fact

International surveys of corporate treasurers have suggested that the main benchmarks for foreign exchange transaction exposure are spot, forward cover and budgeted rate spread equally amongst companies. In many cases the application of these benchmarks is simple and relatively arbitrary. A cynical view would be that the performance measurement yardstick most often used in practice, though seldom explicitly, is based on judgement after the fact given the more favourable of the forward rate and the spot rate available at the time of exchange.

Ready-reckoner charts can be created to suggest choice of hedge, given the performance measurement yardstick, risk-bearing capacity, and the treasurer's spot rate out-turn views. Risk-shy managers mirror their yardsticks. They fully cover forward foreign exchange exposures if measured versus a forward cover yardstick. Risk-shy treasurers keep their loans and deposits on short-term maturities if their measurement criterion so encourages. The risk lover behaves as though he has unlimited capital at his disposal and full autonomy. Risk managing treasurers will not adopt such extreme positions. They will lean towards OTM or ITM options subject to yardstick.

The ready reckoner charts could provide the basis for an examination by the firm's treasury committee of its objectives, policies and strategies. Measurement versus spot, forward or an ATM option are but three special cases. In setting a yardstick, motivation must be balanced by discipline and control.

And finally . . .

Given the two-way risk nature of derivatives such as forward exchange contracts, FRAs (interest rate hedges) and swaps, corporations should carefully consider the selection of their counterparties. They should establish credit lines for banks subject to the bank's creditworthiness. Furthermore, just as the Bank for International Settlements in Basle (BIS) is requiring banks to set aside capital for dealings in derivatives, corporations should allocate reserves against derivative transactions in relation to their bank's credit rating.

CHAPTER

10

Legal risk management
(by Iona Levine)

The market

Recent figures published by the BIS demonstrate that the global market in OTC derivatives continues its rapid expansion. The notional amount of outstanding OTC contracts as at June 1998 stood at USD70 trillion, up 130 per cent on a comparable survey undertaken in May 1995. Set within this context, no book addressing the derivatives markets would be complete without an understanding of the legal risk management issues which are embedded in such dealings.

The market turmoil in 1998 which began in Russia and threatened to undermine the world's developed economies highlighted the importance of a sound legal risk management policy and although most institutions have now implemented robust policies to tackle credit risk, market risk and operational risk, legal risk is often in danger of being overlooked.

Legal risk defined

At its most basic, legal risk is the risk that a particular transaction does not produce the economic results that a party had bargained for, either because there has been a change in law or regulation or more usually because the party failed to appreciate or address one or more of the risks inherent in the transaction. There is a common perception that the legal risks are always linked to the 'complex nature of derivative products', but many of the legal risks assumed by institutions are of the most basic type and apply equally to a variety of derivative and non-derivative transactions. The difference lay in the fact that the derivatives markets are staffed by risk takers rather than those that are risk-averse, and there is therefore a natural reluctance to focus on legal risk, and an even greater reluctance to turn down a transaction because of legal risk. Even in those institutions (of which there are few) which purport to identify and address legal risk, there is a general belief that what was considered to be a legal risk six months or a year ago will shortly cease to be a legal risk as parties become 'more comfortable with the risk'. It is as if legal risks drift in and out of fashion and miraculously disappear when wishful thinking is employed!

'Capturing, analyzing and addressing legal risk is more than simply consulting internal/external lawyers with regard to the risk of a particular transaction.'

Capturing, analyzing and addressing legal risk is more than simply consulting internal/external lawyers with regard to the risk of a particular transaction. It is an appreciation of the risks which an institution is prepared to run and the consequences of taking the risk. Despite the scepticism of the previous paragraphs, it should not be the business of a proactive lawyer to prevent their clients from taking risks but to assist them in identifying, assessing and grading the risk and whilst the risk is important the consequences are even more important.

The consequences are many and various, they range from the unenforceability of a transaction, series of transactions, through to regulatory sanctions, bad publicity and criminal penalties. Whilst market risk and credit risk are factored into the pricing of a transaction, few if any have ever thought of pricing legal risk, yet not to have a sound legal risk management policy whenever an institution fails to execute a master agreement, obtain, review and implement up-to-date legal opinions, and understand the legal environment in which it is taking and placing collateral, is taking a legal risk which should be reflected in the pricing.

Legal risk management and the matrix approach

Legal risk essentially breaks down into:

- the risks of a particular type of transaction
- the risks of the proposed transaction
- documentation risk
- certain less obvious risks, the most notable of which is corporate culture risk.

The majority of legal risks which arise out of OTC derivatives trading can be captured by employing the legal risk matrix set out in this chapter. The matrix divides the legal issues into four inter-related sections:

- counterparty risk
- product risk
- documentation risk
- other risks.

Counterparty risk

In most jurisdictions, derivatives regulation imposes requirements on institutions dealing with certain types of counterparty to 'know their client'. It is therefore axiomatic that the first part of this risk matrix should stress the importance of knowing more than the name of the counterparty for the following reasons:

Ultra vires/*capacity issues*

During the 1990s major financial institutions become acutely aware of the risks which they were assuming by failing to check whether a particular type of counterparty could enter into derivatives. The institutions had entered into derivatives transactions with local authorities and had either not checked whether the local authorities possessed the legal capacity to enter into the transactions or because of the complexity of the legislation had considered the issue and drawn the wrong conclusion. Other financial institutions wrongly believed that local authorities were ultimately backed up with the creditworthiness of the British Government and applied a quasi legal/moral analysis to the situation.

The leading case which highlights this issue is Hazell v Hammersmith & Fulham London Borough Council, House of Lords 1991 2 WLR P372. Regardless of subsequent developments, the case acts as a salutary reminder to parties that they must check that their counterparty has the legal capacity to enter into the particular types of transactions which are being contemplated.

Certain entities may have limited capacity to enter into derivatives transactions; these limitations may relate to the type of transaction, the currency of the transaction, the volume of the transactions or the purpose of a transaction. A party which intends to transact business with entities which have a limited capacity to undertake such business must ensure that they have the tools to monitor that particular restriction, otherwise they are assuming an unnecessary legal risk.

For example, there are investment schemes in the UK referred to in the Financial Services (Regulated Schemes) Regulations 1991, two of which are not permitted to enter into derivatives transactions, whilst four are entitled to do so solely for the purposes of Efficient Portfolio Management as defined in the regulations. Parties get the regulations wrong at their peril.

It is therefore important at the outset to understand the type of legal entity with which you are dealing, for example, whether it is an individual, bank, company, partnership, insurance company, a fund, or a municipality. The jurisdiction in which the counterparty is organized or incorporated is also of paramount importance, as the laws and regulations which determine whether a particular type of entity can enter into a derivatives transaction will usually be the laws and regulations of the country of organization or incorporation of that entity: so, for example, if you wished to consider whether pension funds organized under the laws of Holland had the capacity to transact swaps, you would need to consider Dutch law.

Principal/agent

In order to ensure that all legal risks are accurately captured, it is important to determine whether a party is acting as a principal or an agent, and if acting as an agent the extent of liability (if any) which the agent is prepared to assume. Parties who merely assume without further investigation that the legal and credit risk in respect of all trading is that of the agent are optimists.

There are a variety of ways in which the agency business is conducted in these markets:

(i) the agent discloses the name and full details of the principal to the financial institution and the financial institution conducts its own credit and legal due diligence in respect of the principal: the substantive legal risk has then been assumed by the financial institution; or

(ii) the agent discloses the name and details of the principal to the financial institution but does not provide sufficient information to enable the financial institution to conduct its own credit and legal due diligence. Unless properly addressed by a clear allocation of responsibilities, this practice can give rise to legal risk for both the financial institution and the agent: the financial institution may be relying upon the agent to undertake the due diligence and yet the agent may not have the inclination or resources to undertake the due diligence; or

(iii) the least prudent of all methods for allowing an agent to undertake business is where an agent is dealing on behalf of an unnamed client. In these circumstances an agent simply states that it is acting on behalf of a client but is not prepared to disclose the identity of the client. A financial institution may very well require the agent to execute a side letter indemnifying the institution against the losses which it may suffer as a result of entering into transactions on an unnamed basis. The text of the letter is of course of importance, but the frequency with which such letters are issued and the due diligence which an agent undertakes before it issues such a letter raise wider risk issues. It is easy to conceive of a situation in which an agent issues a significant number of such letters without undertaking any due diligence, the indemnities are called upon and a systemic risk is created.

In response to regulatory pressures and requirements the trend is now towards disclosing the name of the client, but only to a limited number of people within the financial institution, e.g., legal and credit.

Product risks

The exponential growth in OTC derivatives has been largely due to the increased use of two key mitigation techniques, which can be utilized to reduce internal credit requirements and regulatory capital requirements and so free up capital and jealously guarded credit lines:

- netting
- collateralization.

Netting

The type of netting which I am referring to is bilateral close-out netting which ensures that all dealings between the parties can be viewed on a net rather than a gross basis. In short, this means that where two institutions have entered into a series of transactions (e.g., 25 swap transactions) and one of the institutions becomes insolvent or commits another event of default, then the non-defaulting party can close out all outstanding

'The legal enforceability of netting is essentially based upon the insolvency law in the jurisdiction of incorporation of the counterparty.'

transactions and pay or receive the net sum ('netting').

If the netting was not legally effective and the defaulting party had become insolvent, then the non-defaulting party could have found themselves in a situation in which:

(i) they were prevented from closing out the transactions because an insolvency event of default had occurred; or

(ii) they were entitled to close out all 25 transactions, but not to 'net', so that if 10 of the transactions were profitable to the defaulting party, and 15 profitable to the non-defaulting party, then the non-defaulting party would be required to pay across the closing gains in respect of the 10 transactions to the defaulting party, and the non-defaulting party would be left to prove in the liquidation of the defaulting party for the non-defaulting party's gains on the 15 profitable contracts.

I do not propose to discuss the legal risk management issues inherent in netting in any great detail, because the approach which the markets adopt to netting is now quite sophisticated. This is overwhelmingly due to the stringent but practical requirements of the regulators who have the ability to grant or withhold capital relief for netting, and the efforts of trade bodies such as ISDA and the BBA who have operated valuable opinion-gathering exercises and lobbied successfully for legislative change in those jurisdictions which were not conducive to netting.

The legal enforceability of netting is essentially based upon the insolvency law in the jurisdiction of incorporation of the counterparty. This means that before an institution can net, it will need to consider a written and reasoned legal opinion from a reputable external law firm who are equipped to advise upon derivatives and the insolvency law in the jurisdiction of incorporation of the counterparty.

When considering such an opinion (whether it has been provided by ISDA, BBA, any other trade organization, or whether it has been commissioned by the institution itself), it is necessary to ensure that:

- it covers the precise type of entity with whom the institution wishes to net. For example, it should be noted that the ISDA English Jurisdiction opinion expressly excludes amongst other categories of counterparty, building societies, trusts and insurance companies; and
- the opinion covers all of the products which the parties are likely to transact and which they wish to net.

The residual legal risk management issues which appear, arise as a result of:

- the institution failing to ensure that the opinion covers the particular type of institution with whom it wishes to transact business;
- parties failing to realize that not all products are equal for the purposes of netting legislation. Netting legislation in many jurisdictions is very product-specific and unless the products which the parties wish to transact are specifically covered by the netting legislation, the netting may be unenforceable. An effective legal risk management policy should also capture new products and ensure that these are recognized for netting purposes only if they are specifically addressed in the original opinion or a supplementary opinion;
- the institution failing to implement the opinion provider's recommendations, e.g., if the opinion provider recommends that certain specific Japanese events of default should be included in the documentation and this recommendation is not implemented, then this could undermine the enforceability of such netting.

Collateralization

Although collateralization has been the cornerstone of all exchange-traded markets there has been an explosion in the use of collateral in the bilateral OTC markets, which are currently ill-equipped to deal with the issues. Whilst institutions through their exchange-traded dealings and their banking division were familiar with the legal principles related to taking and granting collateral, there have been several developments which push the whole area of collateralization to the top of the list for those concerned with legal risk management.

It is the internationalization of collateral which is responsible for highlighting this area as an important issue coupled with the turnaround times dictated by the market and the market's initial unwillingness to see this as an area of risk. In many quarters there was little or no appreciation that ill-conceived risk mitigation techniques could be responsible for increasing rather than reducing risk.

Since the Asian and Russian cases (which gave parties the opportunity to test current practices and procedures), a number of very valuable reports have been published which summarize the legal and other risks inherent in taking collateral. In particular the *OTC Derivatives Settlement Procedures and Counterparty Risk Management Report*, Basle, September 1998 recognizes the issues when it states:

> The primary legal risk associated with collateral is the risk that the collateral agreement might not be enforceable. The collateral taker must conduct due diligence to ensure that the collateral agreement constitutes a valid and binding agreement. The collateral taker also needs to determine what law governs the creation, perfection and priority of a security interest and whether the applicable law imposes any technical requirements that must be met to make the security interest enforceable. Finally, the collateral taker needs to review the law governing the collateral provider's insolvency and determine whether it can enforce its security interest upon the provider's insolvency. These issues can be complex even when only a single legal jurisdiction is relevant, and this complexity is compounded in cross-border agreements, which are quite common.

Particularly in the area of taking security over securities, it is arguable that current laws do not allow secured creditors to determine with certainty and predictability the substantive law that will govern their rights and obligations.

There has been a general call for law reform in order to assist the markets and prevent a disaster. The EU has recently responded by stating that the mutual acceptance and enforceability of cross-border collateral is indispensable for the stability of the EU financial system. The commission has announced that it will begin its work on collateral in autumn 1999 and anticipates that the relevant directive will be adopted by 2003. Whilst this is to be welcomed, the markets cannot stand still and in the interim each institution will need to design a sophisticated legal risk management policy for collateral.

Gambling

This was of key concern at the beginning of the derivatives markets, but over time as a result of opinions, legislative amendments and market confidence, it ceased to be a fashionable risk. It made a brief return last year when a Moscow Court ruled that non-deliverable forwards were best viewed as gambling contracts under Chapter 58 of the Russian Civil Code and non-binding.

Product life cycle and globalization

The extent and type of legal risk management which is required depends upon where a product is in its particular life cycle. When a product is initially structured, it requires a significant amount of legal input and detailed risk management, which it would ordinarily receive in most institutions. A new products committee is a very valuable tool in ensuring that legal risks have been fully addressed.

Once the product becomes commoditized and provided that it has been properly 'handed over' to an appropriate documentation unit or transaction management team, unless the product is particularly risky or unless it is being sold to less sophisticated investors, it should require very little legal risk management. The product may very well acquire 'bolt-ons' which need to be considered or it could 'go global'.

One of the most important risks to be addressed which is prone to being overlooked is the legal position in respect of that particular product when it begins to get transacted in other jurisdictions. An institution must not assume that what is legally acceptable and enforceable in one jurisdiction will necessarily be legally acceptable and enforceable in another jurisdiction and there are a number of additional matters which need to be addressed over and above the obvious regulatory issues.

Documentation risks

Although the derivatives markets operate on the basis of standard form documentation for most products and although there are no regulatory requirements to complete the documentation prior to trading, but only a requirement that parties should aim to put the documentation in place within three months of the first deal being struck, there is still a notable reluctance to execute documentation on a timely basis, and negotiations often drag on for a disappointingly long period.

> *'An institution must not assume that what is legally acceptable and enforceable in one jurisdiction will necessarily be legally acceptable and enforceable in another jurisdiction . . .'*

No legal risk management policy would be complete without a thorough review of the documentation unit, its practices and procedures, its method of operating and in particular the way in which it links in with credit, legal, operations and the traders. If the documentation is wrong, not sufficiently robust, or unsigned, then the institution's legal protections are significantly undermined.

At the moment there is an alarming but contradictory approach to documentation:

(i) there is an overwhelming backlog of unsigned Master Agreements which are being negotiated to the death, sometimes with good cause, but more often because both parties are insisting on their own standard language. This may very well be because they are not sufficiently trained to recognize that the other party's language produces the same legal result; or because they suffer from the 'not invented here' syndrome. In either event this does nothing to reduce risk, promote netting and must be actively discouraged.

(ii) there is also an over-reliance on standard form documentation, particularly in the confirmations area; this has caused particular difficulties in the area of credit derivatives.

Other risks

Litigation risks

At its most basic, litigation risk is the risk that a counterparty could institute proceedings against an institution, succeed in those proceedings and recover damages. The case could be an isolated matter or it could lead to a flood of cases which the institution would be well-advised to settle. The damages may or may not be substantial in themselves but the cost of management time, and the damage to the institution and the careers of those within that institution could be significant. It may also provoke a regulatory investigation and all of this could in turn lead to the truncation or demise of what was once a great institution. If you think that this is alarmist, you only need to consider the past decade which has seen an increased willingness to litigate on the part of those parties which sustain large losses when the value of derivative transactions move against them. The majority of the cases were instituted in the US and some were settled out of court.

The *causes célèbres* in this area are:

● *Gibson Greeting v Bankers Trust*, began in 1994, settled out of court for USD23 million;

● *Procter and Gamble v Bankers Trust*, began in 1994, settled out of court; the settlement ultimately left Bankers Trust bearing 83 per cent of the losses;

- Orange County, a US municipality with an economy that ranked 28th in the world, filed for bankruptcy for itself and its investment pools and subsequently instituted proceedings against Merrill Lynch and others, claiming amounts in the region of USD2 billion;
- *Bankers Trust v PT Dharmala Sakti Sejahtera, 1995*: this was heard in the commercial court in England where Bankers Trust were successful, and were awarded USD65 million plus interest.

Although there is of course no substitute for reading the individual cases, and different legal systems were involved (various US States laws and English law), the complaints were of a similar type, and there is a common theme which can best be summarized as:

- you (the institution) should have warned me (the client) of the risk; I was relying upon you to do so; we were not dealing at arm's length;
- the product was so complex and customized that only you could have valued it;
- the valuation which you provided was inaccurate, wrong, misleading; you knew that we would rely upon it in preparing our financial statements.

Most financial institutions have implemented a robust sales practices and procedures policy to address the real and perceived legal issues which arise out of the 'mis-selling of derivatives'. However as memories are notoriously short in the derivatives market, particularly when margins are tight, there is of course a risk that the policies will fall by the wayside. This risk is not considered to be fashionable at the moment, largely because there has been an absence of new headline-grabbing litigation. Even without the benefit of a crystal ball, it is clear that credit derivatives is the area which is ripe for litigation. It is quite clear that many less sophisticated users did not fully appreciate the risks which they were assuming when they were purchasing credit derivatives (particularly those which were combined with less than transparent plays on the rouble or when they were credit default options dressed up as notes) and this serves as a reminder that it is not good business practice to sell 'toxic waste' to less sophisticated parties, however attractive such toxic waste appears at the time.

Regulatory risks

Regulatory risk is a form of legal risk. Common examples of this risk are as follows:

- The financial institution is not entitled to transact a particular type of product with a particular type of counterparty for regulatory reasons which should not be confused with the *ultra vires*/capacity issues discussed above. This could be because the financial institution does not have the licences to conduct this type of business in that particular jurisdiction, or because the regulatory regime takes the view that financial institutions should not be allowed to provide OTC derivatives to certain types of entity. Regulatory risk also links in with product risk; there has been much discussion in various jurisdictions as to whether credit derivatives are insurance contracts, and if they are, whether they can only be provided by insurance companies rather than banks.

- Sensitivity to the regulatory environment in which an institution is operating is also of paramount importance. Examples are legendary, the most recent of which is the current regulatory difficulties faced by Credit Suisse, who were alleged to have been using derivative transactions to help Japanese clients to 'window-dress' their accounts. What may be considered to be a perfectly legitimate use of derivatives in certain operating environments, and actively encouraged as a creative approach to balance sheet management, may give rise to legal and regulatory difficulties in other jurisdictions or when regulatory concerns change.

Corporate culture risk

For those institutions which employ in-house lawyers, the tone which an institution sets in relation to its legal department has a direct result on that institution's ability to capture and analyze legal risk. Lawyers in this area, often disparagingly referred to as the 'back office', are not seen to be fulfilling a useful function because they are not generating income and are actively discouraged from asking the correct questions; this obviously impairs their ability to capture and analyze legal risk. It is not a question of salary, and it is often the lawyers in the most highly paid positions that are the victims of a culture which require lawyers to prove that they are 'pro-active' by suspending their critical faculties and acting as a rubber stamp. Many institutions pay lip-service to legal risk management and are keen to site their lawyers on the trading floor; without the appropriate protections, this merely exacerbates risk. Legal risk management will rarely if ever be provided by external lawyers in case an unwelcome view leads to allegations of ivory towerness and the loss of a client.

> *'Many institutions pay lip-service to legal risk management and are keen to site their lawyers on the trading floor; without the appropriate protections, this merely exacerbates risk.'*

People risk is an important element in legal risk management. This is of particular concern in the documentation area where headcount constraints have led to an over-reliance on untrained temporary staff. These staff have little grounding in the documentation and even less grounding in the ethics of the institution for which they work. They are encouraged to act as a processing function, despite the fact that they are an important bulwark in controlling risks.

Conclusion

Legal risk cannot be eliminated, but it can be effectively managed. Whilst there are certain institutions that genuinely manage their legal risk because it is perceived as an important plank in managing a well-run business, there are many that do not and will not, unless there is the offer of a carrot or stick. Not only do you need to consider how well your own institution captures, analyzes and addresses legal risk, but you must also be aware of how your counterparties deal with such risks, as failure to address legal risk could result in systemic risk.

Government's view of the economy could be summed up in a few short phrases: If it moves, tax it. If it keeps moving, regulate it. And if it stops moving, subsidize it.

RONALD REAGAN

11

Taxation aspects of derivatives and risk management

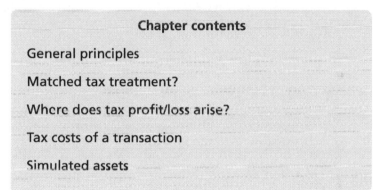

General principles

Tax money is real money. The profit and loss accounts of individual capital market and derivative desks should always be calculated on an after-tax basis, allowing for the time value of tax money to be paid, set-off or recovered.

It is essential to understand the tax rules which apply to the transaction being undertaken. And all the parties must bear in mind that the rules of the game can change during the game or even after the game has finished! Retrospective legislation has been enacted in many countries. Tax avoidance legislation in the UK allows the tax authorities to tax transactions or packages of transactions if they feel that the purpose of the transaction or transactions is to avoid tax.

I must emphasize that tax planning advice is way beyond the scope of this book. I am far from an authority on tax and merely seek to illustrate some principles as I see them. Not only does tax treatment change in any one country from year to year, but it differs from country to country. That, in itself, may prove to be an opportunity for a cross-border transactions. But do not leave the issue of taxation until after you've done the deal. A successful negotiation leading to a benefit of a few basis points can prove to be a Pyrrhic victory if there is a tax loss of several hundred basis points. Believe me, I have seen it happen!

Matched tax treatment?

Character

As already discussed in Chapter 3, 'What drives innovation?', financial cash flows can be manipulated so that their apparent character changes.

If one transaction is treated as income and another matching transaction is regarded as capital by the taxation authorities, and therefore treated differently, then the position is beneficial if any gain is not taxable and any loss tax-deductible. On the other hand, it is bad news if the position is reversed with gains taxable and losses not deductible. Some jurisdictions, for example, do not tax capital gains at all or do not tax gains on government bonds.

By way of example, recall that the break forward was invented in 1985 partly to solve a tax problem. Not only did corporate treasurers, or their finance directors, not want to pay option premiums upfront for the right to buy a currency in the future that they might never exercise, but the UK tax authorities at that time regarded the premiums as wasting assets. There was no tax deduction on premiums for unexercised currency options. So in the course of a particularly fruitful lunch

'. . . financial cash flows can be manipulated so that their apparent character changes.'

with Brian Atkinson, Head of Taxation at Midland Bank's Group Treasury, I created the break forward. The option premium was embedded into the forward.

Transactions conducted in the course of a trade, especially by a financial institution, are more likely to get matching characterization. Outside that safe haven it is possible that the losses on derivatives will not be tax-deductible particularly where they are carried out by individuals.

Timing

If both legs of a matched transaction are marked to market, then any gains and losses will probably match for tax purposes. However, if one is marked to market and the other is taxed on the basis of accruals and realization, then gains and losses may arise in different years. If there are restrictions on carrying back or carrying forward losses then there can be, at worst, a total real mismatch instead of just a timing mismatch. Even where both sides of a transaction are accruals on realization, there can be a mismatch. A realized profit on a hedging transaction cannot strictly, under most tax jurisdictions, be spread forward over the life of the transaction being hedged. Thus unless realization occurs for both, the underlying exposure and the hedge, in the very same tax period, there will be a mismatch.

Place

If the hedges are effected in a different legal entity from the one which carries the hedged transaction, than a loss in one may not be offsettable against the gain in the other, even if both are in the same country. Similarly there can be the same problem where transactions are effected in different branches of the same company, depending on how branch profits are taxed. This is a frequent problem with centralized treasury companies hedging group financial exposures.

Where does tax profit/loss arise?

A centralized group risk management function, based in a different country from the one where the risk lies, can lead to taxation difficulties. The main risk is as discussed above under *Place*. The other tax risk is that if the central risk manager has authority to commit group companies to derivative contracts, and regularly does so, then he is likely to create a taxable branch in the country where he is based, for each group company he represents, in respect of the transactions he conducts for them. It is generally preferable that such a function be a consulting function rather than a 'management' function. Such people should not have the power to contract on behalf of companies. They should merely advise them.

Tax costs of a transaction

VAT and sales tax

Remember that transaction taxes can apply to purchases and sales of goods. An option or forward can therefore potentially give rise to value added tax or sales tax in some form, even where delivery of the physical is never likely to happen. This is a particular concern to those transacting 'Islamic' investments. I was well down the process of concluding a particular Islamic *Murabaha* investment for a client when it occurred to me that value added tax would have been payable on the 'mark-up'. In the hands of an individual not registered for VAT, the value added tax would apply not just to the mark-up but to the entire principal invested!

Insurance and betting

Although it rarely proves to be a problem, there is always concern as to whether taxes on betting, or on insurance contracts, apply to derivative transactions, as all three have similar economic characteristics. But herein lies another problem. There may be little advantage in trying to get a product classified as an insurance policy rather than as a banking contract. Many countries only permit specifically authorized insurance companies to enter into insurance contracts. Entered into by non-insurance company, such a product would be deemed illegal and therefore unenforceable. The same applies to betting. Under gaming laws in many countries, betting is either illegal or is unenforceable.

Withholding tax on swaps

Withholding tax does not normally apply to option premium or net settlement payments. It is more likely to apply to the regular 'interest-related' payments under an interest rate swap. This may especially be the case as the very basis of such a swap, single currency or cross currency, is the interest rate applied to a notional principal sum. Where this happens, the ISDA contract normally requires grossing up or, if a change of law, can result in a break in the contract. Even so, withholding tax is rarely applied to swap interest equalization payments, even though the authorities are aware that this is sometimes used to reduce withholding tax on real borrowing, e.g., low coupon borrowing compared with swaps into high coupon currency. Some jurisdictions might, however, recharacterize such a transaction so that it is treated as a high coupon borrowing.

There should always be preparation against changes in taxation that have a retrospective effect. Two recent cases illustrate the point.

Withholding tax on interest

A European Union proposal, published in May 1998 in draft form, to impose withholding tax on interest income has caused concern in Europe's capital markets. Such a proposal could well drive much eurobond business outside the European Union.

The EU has proposed to introduce a 20 per cent withholding tax on interest income, including interest earned on bank deposits and eurobond holdings. The majority of eurobond issues are structured so that the interest is paid without deduction of tax or is grossed-up by the issuing borrower so that the investor receives the contracted interest. To counter opposition to the withholding tax, an alternative plan was also proposed in the EU draft so that countries would inform other European tax authorities about interest payments to EU citizens in their jurisdictions, with the information being supplied by banks holding investments on behalf of their clients.

In 1989, the EU made a similar move to impose a 15 per cent tax withholding tax on eurobond interest. Combined pressure from London and Luxembourg, the major Euromarket centres managed to kill such proposals. The current move is likewise being opposed by the British authorities and is opposed by the International Securities Market Association, ISMA. ISMA argues that new issue business would move to Switzerland, Bermuda and Singapore. In a July 1999 letter sent by ISMA to its members, it said, 'if adopted in its present form [the directive] would be likely to have disastrous consequences on the economies and the employment levels of the financial centres of the EU. The directive poses a problem not just for London but for the banking and securities industries throughout the EU.' Given the swift development of internet communications, it is likely that financial markets will increasingly gravitate to low-cost centres or those that can provide a taxation haven. Tax authorities have to be careful to ensure that their actions do not reduce the tax collected if corporate profits were caused to be earned outside their jurisdictions.

As far as existing issues are concerned, if issuers are able to do so under the original terms and conditions of the issue, they would redeem their existing issues in the market ahead of schedule to avoid their having to pay the 20 per cent tax on behalf of their investors. Those borrowers with issues with a grossing-up clause, but with no provision to redeem, would have no choice but to bear the increased interest cost or repurchase the bonds in the secondary market. Under all circumstances there would be a considerable increase in legal costs, as investors battle with issuers as to who pays the tax. Then there is the problem of interest rate risk on fixed-rate issues. Depending on when and at what rate the bond was issued, many issuers would seek to use the EU ruling to repay high rate finance and issue new bonds at a lower rate or raise equity.

Withholding tax on equity dividends

When the UK Labour Government came to power in 1997, its first budget changed the tax treatment on equity dividends. Dividends had been paid with a tax credit which could be reclaimed by non-taxpayers.

A problem arose for financial institutions issuing retail equity-linked guaranteed investment schemes. These institutions covered their risks by entering into equity swaps and options with the market. The market, highly competitive by then, assumed that the tax credit would be reclaimable over the life of the guaranteed savings scheme, most of which are five years in term. The change in dividend withholding tax made many such equity derivatives and retail investments unprofitable.

Who the losers were depended on whether the change in taxation was foreseen, and what taxation terms in the derivative structure were agreed between the retail financial institution and the investment bank. There may also have been an appropriate clause in the agreement between the retail financial institution and the saver.

Simulated assets

Equity derivatives are the main area where characterization asymmetry can arise. Stock 'lending' is a misnomer. In the legal sense, counterparty A sells his holding to counterparty B and simultaneously agrees to buy back the same amount of the stock at an agreed future date.

Counterparty B, most likely, uses the stock to fill a short sale. Thus that stock has gone from the balance sheet of A and has not in any sense been 'loaned'. Counterparty A has got a gain or loss on disposal. Any 'dividend' payment he receives from counterparty

B is not really a dividend. It is a cash sum which happens to equate with the dividend forgone by A on sale. Any stock counterparty A receives back is different stock of the same type and not the original. The transfers of stock may be liable to stamp duty.

'Dividends often get unique tax treatment, either as exempt income or because they carry some form of tax credit.'

Such transactions only get back to the form of a 'loan', if there is a law that ensures that treatment. They should not be confused with collateral transactions where stock is placed as security for a loan of cash and there is no change in beneficial ownership. Even under such circumstances, an exchange in nominal ownership can sometimes cause difficulty if the tax authority confuses beneficial and legal ownership, or is vague on the difference between the two.

Dividends often get unique tax treatment, either as exempt income or because they carry some form of tax credit. In the absence of any specific legal provisions, a derivative contract including a payment in lieu of the dividend can never get the same tax treatment as the dividend itself. Such legal provisions, if made, will prescribe the precise type of contract to which concessionary treatment is extended and will often require payment of a withholding or other tax by the payer of the substitute dividend. In such circumstances it may be that payment of a manufactured dividend is not tax deductible.

And finally . . .

Life would, of course, be a lot simpler if all cash flows, in and out, were treated the same in the hands of everyone. A step in the right direction was taken in the 1998 UK budget. Inflation indexation relief for capital gains tax purposes was abolished. It is a pity that capital gains tax itself was not abolished and merged into income tax. In terms of spending power, there is no difference between a capital gain and income.

The moral with the recent cases illustrated is to read and re-read the documentation before entering into any deal. I am no tax authority, but have never bought any financial instrument before endeavouring to understand the implications of the agreement. As a trader or investor, do not delegate responsibility and rely on a lawyer or tax expert. If it is your bottom line that will suffer, it is up to you to make sure that all eventualities are covered. Or take a business risk and go ahead with the deal, viewing a certain possibility as unlikely in the life of the contract, and, if so, within the healthy profit margin that you seek.

And financial products continue to develop with tax considerations in mind. However, tax authorities are increasingly legislating retrospectively to capture tax avoidance schemes.

All you need to advance something is a good imag-
ination and a pile of junk.

THOMAS ALVA EDISON

V

Back to the future:

Current developments and trends

We've seen it all before. Or have we? We have seen three property or real estate cycles in the last quarter-century and are well into another one. The current property boom is likely to also end in tears. However. this part does not provide an economic forecast. Are the current developments in financial product development genuinely new, or are they merely a form of ignorance innovation?

Part V looks at current developments and trends, featuring the new developments of credit derivatives and insurance derivatives. Part V also includes a chapter, 'Dangers and disasters; profits and principles', that looks at financial market ethical issues, and the part closes with some crystal-ball gazing at likely developments with a concluding section, *Less technophilia – have faith in fools*.

The hurricane is not more or less likely to hit because more hurricane insurance has been written. In financial markets this is not true. The more people write financial insurance, the more likely it is that the disaster will happen because the people who know you have sold the insurance can make it happen.

JOHN MERIWETHER,
Long Term Capital Management

CHAPTER

12

Credit and insurance derivatives

Credit derivatives

Introduction

Credit derivatives have stormed on to the market in recent years and have shown exponential growth. The fast-growing credit derivatives market (USD20 billion in 1996 to an expected USD100 billion before 2000) is eerily familiar. Traders are offering pure 'insurance' against a default. But many countries strictly separate banking from insurance business. And credit derivatives are but a small step from credit insurance.

But the business of transferring credit risk is not entirely new. Government bodies such as the UK's Export Credit Guarantee Department have taken on credit risk from exporters for many years. And many insurers provide credit insurance. Even in the purely banking market, credit risk can be transferred through loan participations and assignments.

The development of credit derivatives has raised concerns over the legality of such structures when carried out by banks. Under the UK Insurance Companies Act 1982, only companies authorized by the Department of Trade and Industry can carry out 'insurance business'. But banks have been writing insurance policies on interest rates (caps) for a decade.

'The markets do not appear to have learned any lessons notwithstanding the long list of derivative disasters.'

Whilst such 'insurance' business may have caused banks a few problems, the business has been quite legal under the UK Financial Services Act 1986. It is regarded as 'investment business' and not 'insurance business'. But most derivative marketers, when explaining caps to clients, have quite correctly referred to them as 'interest rate insurance policies'.

The UK financial law panel paper on the point more or less suggested that all of the regulators should get together and decide how to regulate the business. Nobody would then take issue if all of the regulators were agreed.

Most people have no idea of how this scenario will play out in other legal jurisdictions. It appears that bankers are taking the same approach to doing business that they did with local authority swaps. A decade ago, the London Hammersmith & Fulham local authority wrote interest rate caps that were later declared *ultra vires* transactions. The markets do not appear to have learned any lessons notwithstanding the long list of derivative disasters. There may very well be an insurance company which decides to protect its own patch; or an overseas regulator of a bank or a securities house which challenges an institution's transactions; or perhaps an insolvency practitioner will take the point and refuse to settle on a credit derivative that he believes is an insurance product; or a firm that has simply lost money on a credit derivative and seeks to squirm out of its obligations.

Whilst not seeking to generate another bout of 'Derivatiphobia', it appears that in order to ensure that transactions are generated, the market has developed collective amnesia and is prepared to build a huge global position based on shifting sands.

Apparently some Asian bankers in branches overseas were invited to sell credit default swaptions in the autumn of 1997. These bankers were under considerable pressure from head office to increase off-balance sheet income and they jumped at the chance of generating fee income. There is the faintest suspicion that on selling their national credit, Western bankers felt free to call in their underlying loans or play hardball in the negotiations.

Credit derivatives show all of the usual signs that have characterized other segments of the derivatives market at the stages when they achieved explosive growth. New products are being introduced at a fast rate. Each issue of the derivatives trade papers reports that another dealer or broker has entered the market or has hired a team and that another important end-user is incorporating credit derivatives into its strategy. Individual dealer and dealer associations are working to produce standard documents for credit derivatives which can achieve market acceptance. Regulators of key participants in this market have adapted their rules to accommodate this product.

Overview

The objectives of the various participants in the credit derivatives market are diverse and, as with all derivatives markets, often diametrically opposed. Hedgers may be prepared to take on specific credit risks in order to neutralize other existing risks in their portfolios or they may be sellers of these specific credit risks.

Banks and other financial institutions that generate most of the major syndicated loans often use credit derivatives to manage the credit risk of particular borrowers in their portfolio of assets. A lender which is a participant in the syndicated loan and corporate debt markets must commit to large participations in new borrowings, and then quickly sub-underwrite or sell on its share in each new borrowing. Credit derivatives are financial instruments which can be used along with more traditional techniques such as loan syndication and securitization to reduce a lender's credit exposure to individual borrowers and therefore its capital requirements for the loans. It can pass on the risk of default on credit derivatives.

Credit derivatives can occasionally be more efficient than selling down participations or creating assignments. This is because market segmentation leads to differential pricing opportunities. And some ready buyers of credit derivatives are not active in the loan market. Usually in loan participations, a lender is obliged to disclose to the borrower if the loan is sold on in any form. However, using a credit derivative, the lender retains full loan rights and obligations and maintains the relationship with the borrower who is none the wiser if the lender chooses to offload the risk into the market. A sale of a loan also usually requires obligations on the primary lender to relay information on the borrower and obtain approvals to changes in terms.

From a credit derivatives buyer perspective, relatively poor credits with high borrowing costs can 'lend' to good credits without suffering a running loss. After all a derivative is a contract for differences and whose value reflects future *changes* in value and not absolute values.

Investment fund and insurance company investors also find credit derivatives attractive in obtaining high yields. Many suitable credits do not issue bonds. And the collateral backing the credit can be superior in the case of a credit derivative. Credit derivatives can also be highly leveraged and highly structured to maximize exposure. Such investors also may not want to handle the administration involved in a loan participation.

Definition of a credit derivative

In general, a credit derivative is a derivative, that is to say a forward, swap or option or similar instrument, in which one or both parties' payments are based on the payments under or revaluation of a loan or bond.

This definition can be extended to include payments on baskets of loans and bonds. It also includes a note or bond with an embedded credit derivative.

Just as a currency forward or swap can transfer just the foreign exchange exposure element of a bond to a third party, a credit derivative can eliminate just the credit risk component on a bond and retain all other aspects of the particular bond. Simplistically, credit risk is the risk of default of a particular asset, which may, in itself be a function of a host of other risks such as currency and interest rate risk. The credit risk premium is the price of a particular credit risk. It is not just a function of a particular borrower, but is dependent on particular borrowing instruments issued by an entity. The premium will vary depending on the particular terms of a borrowing. It serves to illustrate the definition with a few examples.

Types of credit derivatives

The market is rapidly developing and this list is no doubt out of date as I write. These are some standard types of credit derivative.

Loan portfolio swaps

These can diversify the risk on commercial bank portfolios in the same way as insurance companies re-insure their portfolios. HSBC may wish to diversify out of Far Eastern risk and BSCH may wish to spread the risk of its Latin American portfolio. HSBC and BSCH could swap with each other payments received on a specified basket of each bank's outstanding loans, thereby reducing the regional concentration risk and therefore the credit risk of their loan portfolios.

Total return swaps

These are one-way transfers of credit risk as opposed to the two-way credit risk exchange under loan portfolio swaps. Similar to such swaps in the commodity or equity markets, under a total return swap, ABC pays the interest and fees generated by a specified basket of credits. In return, BCA pays LIBOR plus a margin. In addition, the basket of credits is marked to market. ABC pays any increase in the market value; BCA pays any decrease in the market value of the credits. By way of example, ABC would pay to BCA the interest paid on a particular bond issued by DEF plus the increase in value of the bond. BCA would pay to ABC, LIBOR plus 4 per cent, and any decrease in value of the bond. The revaluation transfer is relatively simple for liquid bonds with a transparent open market price. However, many credit derivatives are written on illiquid instruments. Extreme caution must be exercised when entering into such derivatives, as there is considerable scope for either party to manipulate the value of the underlying just before the fixing dates.

Credit default options

These are closest to the traditional credit insurance instruments and cause the most concern in jurisdictions that strictly separate banking and insurance.

ABC pays BCA an agreed 'insurance' premium in advance or through the life of the contract for BCA's obligation to pay to ABC a formulated payment on a specified credit event on the underlying instrument issued by a particular borrower. The credit event may not necessarily be a default, but may be a deterioration in credit beyond a certain benchmark. The credit event benchmark may even not be a real default, but a perceived deterioration in credit by certain rating agencies in the form of a specific rating downgrade. On the triggering of a credit event, BCA makes the formulated payment, perhaps the difference between the notional principal amount under the contract and the new market value. The credit event may also be a delayed payment. Again care must be exercised to guard against the counterparty's ability to activate the credit event.

> 'Credit default instruments may take the form of swaps or options.'

Credit default instruments may take the form of swaps or options. Swaps imply two-way gains and benefits. If the credit risk deteriorates, the BCA pays ABC. If the credit risk improves, then ABC pays BCA.

In the case of credit options, on the triggering of a credit event, settlement may be by actual delivery of the asset at a pre-determined price, usually par. In the case of credit options on a basket, the trigger could be with respect to just one component of the basket or to a certain percentage of the basket of bonds or loans.

Credit-linked notes

These are strictly not derivatives, but are cash instruments based on derivatives. Some such credit-linked notes have embedded credit derivatives. Very often the point is to generate a high-yielding investment instrument. In exchange for paying a higher rate of interest the issuer, often a special purpose vehicle, has the right to reduce the principal amount of the note subject to certain specified credit events. The issuer pays a variable interest and/or principal based on the occurrence or non-occurrence of certain credit events involving a specified borrower.

For example, an investor may only be permitted to make investments with a small list of authorized AA and above issuers. Furthermore, he may have a certain target for income at a level above LIBOR. His investment position is not marked to market. A special purpose vehicle could buy the approved investments and then issue a note where the interest rate deteriorates should *any one* of the constituent instruments suffer a credit event. The notes are backed by the AA or better bonds. A credit event on any one instrument is more likely to occur than the deterioration of the average credit. Thus the investor obtains a higher yield than the average yield on the underlying instruments, but has a greater probability of price deterioration than any individual instrument in the basket. But the possible deterioration in value is a future manager's problem. This is a classic case of an instrument being developed to satisfy regulation arbitrage and generate bonuses for a manager as a result of inadequate management accounting.

Other credit derivative products traded include options, forwards and swaps on the market interest rate spread versus the interest rate on government risk equivalents. A common occurrence in credit derivatives with option-like characteristics is the presence of an insurance element. As has already been mentioned, this causes regulatory nervousness because of the separation of insurance and banking in many jurisdictions.

Special features of credit derivatives

- In many credit derivatives, the creditworthiness of the credit derivative counterparty, with the resulting probability that it will meet its obligations under the credit derivative, adds another level of credit risk which must be analyzed. Credit limits should be established for each derivative counterparty, so as to avoid concentration of risk with one such institution. The added credit risk would be similar to that under other derivatives – the current exposure measured by the mark-to-market replacement cost of the transaction plus an estimate of the potential future exposure of the transaction to market price changes. Given that market price is difficult to obtain, this in itself is not easy.

- Credit derivatives are notably less liquid than many other standard interest-rate and currency derivatives. This is particularly so if they are highly structured or incorporate credit risks not commonly held. It is likely that any credit derivative would be considerably less liquid than a loan or bond on the underlying credit. Price is highly dependent on liquidity. When the credit position is unwound, an investor may find that realized value is far from the value in the equivalent loan market. This risk must be watched closely in transactions likely to be terminated before expiry. Purchasing a 'used' credit derivative requires vigilance on all the applicable credit risks.

- Continuous loan spread information on particular borrowers is not readily available, for the simple reason that loans are seldom traded and prices are not established on a minute-by-minute basis as is the case for bonds. Measuring price risk for credit derivatives is therefore a good deal more complicated than for some other derivatives because of sparse historical data available.

- A bank holding a loan asset on a particular borrower may seek to unwind that position with a credit derivative on a bond issued by the same entity. However, the credit risk and volatility of bonds is quite different from that on loans, and therefore there is a significant basis risk consideration. This is the principle behind the long-standing existence of the asset swap market. Bonds tend to be much more volatile than loans and therefore asset swappers buy such over-depreciated assets, attach swaps to them to convert them to floating-rate, loan-like packages and then sell them at higher yields than loans.

● The market reflects the early stages of the derivatives market in the non-standard nature of both the instruments and documentation. There is a trend, however, to standardization.

● Major moral hazards lie in the close relationship between the parties influencing credit derivatives and the underlying credits. The market is far from transparent and those writing such derivatives are often not independent. In particular if one of the counterparties is the calculation agent, then that party has won considerable financial power and perhaps the ability to influence the outcome. Most credit derivatives are transacted between banks, and therefore disputes can usually be resolved amicably. However, weaker banks must take care not to be overawed and they should be adamant in insisting on an equitable dispute resolution process.

> *'It is of paramount importance that the credit event itself is defined clearly and fairly, so as to avoid disputes.'*

● It is of paramount importance that the credit event itself is defined clearly and fairly, so as to avoid disputes. Transactions may include several credit events from a credit rating downgrade to a default by the underlying borrower on a different liability or a 'cross default' event. A trigger may also be an event of restructuring of the underlying loans. But what if the underlying asset is restructured for some trivial reason such as change of name as a result of merger? A non-material adverse event may be used by a counterparty to trigger a credit event. The occurrence of a credit event may be difficult to verify. Clear procedures must establish whether a credit event actually occurs with independent evidence.

- Lenders receive valuable confidential information from borrowers. If that information is not passed on to credit derivative counterparties, then such entities are placed at a significant disadvantage compared to those with access to the information. However, such confidential information may well cause a disorderly market in the borrower's liabilities. So generally credit events are only publicly announced ones.

- Credit risk evaluation, and therefore capital backing, is made complicated when a limited transfer of risk occurs on a sliding scale.

Conclusion

Over the past few years, many of the difficulties associated with credit derivatives have either been solved or ignored and the market has continued its rapid growth. Instruments are becoming more standardized, as is documentation. Furthermore, the regulatory bodies seem to be looking favourably on such instruments.

Credit risk derivatives have an established place in the financial instrument panel; but only if extreme care is exercised. The dangers of abuse, miscalculation and legal risks inherent are far greater than those of now traditional derivative instruments.

Caveat emptor.

Insurance derivatives

Bancassurance

There has been an overlap between the banking and capital markets industries and insurance businesses for some time, but the two branches of finance have been growing ever closer together – and not just in the form of bancassurance groups such as Lloyds bank and ING Group. With the emergence in the United Kingdom of Scottish Widows Bank, Prudential Bank, Midland Life and Britannia Life, the distinction between insurance, banking and building society business has been blurred and to me seems anachronistic. So as to avoid artificial regulatory problems, there should just be all-purpose financial institutions with supervision based on risk-adjusted capital base and shareholder approval with protection for retail clients.

Overview

The major drift together of banking and insurance has taken place since the development of derivatives in the early 1980s. Despite the fact that interest rate caps and currency options are clearly insurance products, legislation in jurisdictions with strict separation of the businesses has declared such financial insurance lines to be banking. Credit derivatives could also be deemed to be insurance products. But since the mid-1990s, corporate risk managers and insurance companies began to look to the capital derivatives markets for more effective ways to hedge their general insurance risks. And investment banks which had found their margins falling in the capital markets began to cast an eagle eye over what they saw as attractive margins in the re-insurance industry.

> *'The major drift together of banking and insurance has taken place since the development of derivatives in the early 1980s.'*

This convergence of banking and insurance has led to the generation of a number of new financial instruments that utilize the properties of structures in both markets.

Example

Consider a general insurance company A-Sure that has suffered significant losses as a result of hurricanes. It could purchase a form of insurance derivative called a contingent capital facility to complement its catastrophe re-insurance programme. This facility is very similar to a traditional financial derivatives barrier or trigger option.

In the contingent event of a triggering event being a defined loss through hurricanes large enough to significantly exceed its traditional coverage, A-Sure has the option of issuing a certain pre-specified principal amount of convertible preference shares at predetermined terms to the insurance derivative provider.

This arrangement provides A-Sure with immediate access to funds when called upon to meet its obligations as a result of another hurricane disaster. The insurance derivatives provider has the right to convert the preference shares to ordinary equity. A-Sure can refinance and redeem the shares at any time. Here we have a capital market structure with the strike rate being a traditional re-insurance event, combining elements from both banking and insurance disciplines.

Conclusion

Thus the borders between the two areas have begun to break down as structures move from one area to the other dependent on regulatory preferences and treatment. At present there is still significant market segmentation and there is no continuum of products spanning banking and insurance largely due to regulatory separation. Accordingly there are profits to be made by those institutions that are able to structure and book traditional insurance deals as banking structures, and conversely, treat banking structures as insurance policies. There are differences in taxation, accounting and regulation which allow for innovative financial engineering.

In due course, competition will lead to finer pricing and such hybrid cross-over transactions will become standardized and com-moditized. It will then be time for the innovative bankers and insurance risk managers to move on to other fields. The end-con-sumer, the corporate all-risks manager, will be the ultimate beneficiary as pricing becomes transparent. Meanwhile the flexible bancassurance firms that can skip between both fields will generate the rewards that feature in any new market. But they must also be careful in what is sure to be a regulatory minefield. The real test for this market has yet to come. It will come when a firm loses a sub-stantial sum of money on these hybrid structures for whatever reason and seeks to wriggle out of its obligations.

In business a reputation for honesty and fair dealing is the key to success. If you can fake that, you have got it made!

GROUCHO MARX

Dangers and disasters; profits and principles

Chapter contents

Retail clients

Corporate business

My word is my bond

Some cautionary tales

Conclusion

Over the past decade, a tsunami of disasters purportedly relating to derivatives has washed over the financial markets. Or so it would seem from reports in the press. Complexity in financial markets sometimes leads to strains in ethical standards. There is always the possibility that a relatively simple scam is heavily structured into a complex financial instrument with the sole purpose of confusing the client or the client's management. Because of this complexity it is vital to deal with a firm, bank or corporate you can trust. In short – know your counterparty.

Sometimes it is not the bank that breaks the contract. In the mid-1990s, there were cases where the corporate client alleged that it did not understand the derivatives contract. And this was only after the corporate had profited from earlier contracts. The vast majority of the large losses have had very little to do with derivatives, but derivatives have proved an easy scapegoat.

Retail clients

One fraud has already been illustrated in Chapter 6, 'Derivatives for the retail client'. I reported on how in Spain firms of unscrupulous brokers sold futures investment schemes to small investors. In Albania, the failure of pyramid get-rich-quick schemes led to angry investors. Even in sophisticated markets such as the UK, it is strange indeed that mortgage lending business is outside the scope of regulation by the Financial Services Act. A UK government 'announcement' on future regulation is expected in early 2000. Structured derivatives-linked savings products have been launched, with inadequate training given to staff in an attempt to keep costs down.

The next time you see a mortgage advertisement, ring up and ask for an explanation and justification of the mortgage annual percentage rate (APR) quoted. You'll get a straight answer, of course, but not much help. I recently saw an interesting quasi-fixed rate mortgage product advertised by a UK bank. I entered in some details into an Excel spread sheet and attempted to cross-check the APR that the advertisement quoted. On failing to get an answer close to the quoted rate, I phoned the customer service number quoted. A very pleasant voice told me: 'I am sorry I cannot tell you. It just comes off the computer print-out. And I can't get a computer print-out without entering full details of the property you wish to mortgage along with your salary details.'

In the case of retail clients, regardless of the strict legal position, we have plenty of examples of adverse publicity destroying a business. So extra care must be taken when launching new retail financial instruments with embedded derivatives. In my opinion,

> *'ring up and ask for an explanation and justification of the mortgage annual percentage rate (APR) quoted.'*

it is advisable to launch these via the internet only, so that any technical queries can be answered by competent staff via e-mail and then added to the Frequently Asked Questions WebPages.

Corporate business

In terms of corporate business, there have been a few instances in the derivatives market where a financial institution deliberately sought to mislead a corporate client about a contract. But if the client is an execution-only purchaser of a financial product from a bank rather than being advised by the investment bank, the onus is on the client to satisfy himself that at the agreed price, the contract is appropriate for his firm. If a bank selling a structure makes an 'unhealthy' or 'excessive' profit out of a transaction, is it necessarily unjustified? If the structure, in the considered opinion of the purchasing corporate client, reduces its risk or is appropriate to its financing or investment needs, then it is in its own interests to value the transaction from its own perspective. The perspective and profitability of the selling bank is only relevant in so far as knowledge of the bank's valuation and pricing methods might aid in the negotiation of terms or the construction of the product by alternative means. The ingenuity of an investment bank required to come up with desirable financial instruments has to be paid for.

If an investment bank shows a proprietary product to a corporate client, is it acceptable for the client to show the product to other banks for pricing purposes? No, it is not acceptable without the express permission of the bank offering the product. Pricing of financial products is not particularly complicated. It is the identification of the problem or opportunity that is the most valuable. But current legal developments should make the protection of financial product intellectual property rights more secure.

My word is my bond

All too often now if a man says his word is his bond, one would be well advised to insist on taking his bond.

SIR ANTHONY GRANT MP,
in the debate on the UK Financial Services Bill

'My word is my bond' seemingly just does not apply to the financial markets as it used to. There are cases where a sale price is agreed when the market is distressed. And then when the market improves the seller has sought to renegotiate the price. In some cultures this is deemed to be quite ethical on the grounds that the original price was agreed under duress and therefore unfair.

Cutting out the middle-man

Fifteen years ago, as a junior trader at a bank, I concluded a swap transaction with a US bank via a broker. The broker happened to be my firm's US subsidiary. A few weeks later I did another deal direct with the US bank, bypassing the broker. All hell broke out and I was rightly accused of being unprofessional.

What is the relationship between two principals once the first deal is struck via a broker? After how many deals via a broker can one deal direct? Middle-men, brokers and agents perform a very useful service in putting two parties with equal and opposite interests together.

It is useful to draw on parallels with other industries that use intermediaries. Some airlines have sought to set up their own discounting 'agents' under discreet names or more openly sell direct to the public via the internet. Quite naturally this annoys the existing agents who the airlines use to sell their tickets. Depending on your bargaining power, you have to be extremely careful about cutting out intermediaries who may be needed in the future.

Many internet portals and free service providers base their financial plans on an increasing flow of commission income from linked retailers. The retailers soon build up a substantial database of customers through such referrals. Some such stores market direct to 'their' customers via e-mail providing an internet link which bypasses the partners after the initial referrals. They advise partners who complain along the lines of: 'Our intention is not to cut off your relationship with your customer.' But they inconsistently rely on legalese such as: 'Our terms and conditions are clearly stated and you as a partner have agreed those terms . . .' Relationships are not about using legal small print. One internet store said: 'You could compare what you and we do to a cosmetics counter within a department store. You as a specialist have your ways of keeping customers, but that does not preclude us from promoting our extended range of products to any customer who has purchased from our store.' But Chanel, Dior etc, do not build up a database of cosmetics customers gained through department stores and then mail them suggesting that they should deal direct by mail order (and effectively no longer with the department store). No doubt the internet store would be aggrieved if wholesalers, in turn, placed forms in every product suggesting that end-purchasers buy direct from them.

So before using a broker or intermediary establish the ground rules clearly. Would the broker accept direct contact between the introduced clients after the first deal?

Some cautionary tales

Herstatt's forex contracts

One of the earliest cases of unexpected loss in the derivatives market occurred in the foreign exchange markets in June 1974. Spot and contracts are settled for value spot and because of the short time to settlement, most banks did not impose credit limits to cover settlement risk. Settlement risk occurs in spot and forward contracts because different time zones lead to different settlement times for each leg of the currency exchange. The German bank Herstatt had a number of maturing spot and forward contracts where it received D-marks and had to pay out US dollars. Herstatt had run into difficulties. In the six hours after it received the D-marks and had to pay its US dollar obligations in New York, Herstatt went into liquidation.

Tender trap

A particular European bank provided tender to contract foreign exchange contracts. These forward contracts with corporate clients involved the sale of foreign currency against the home currency. There was no option involved but there was conditionality. If the corporate client won the export contract order, then it was obliged to enter into a forward contract to sell the foreign currency for the home currency at the pre-agreed rate even if unfavourable. If the client did not win the contract, then it had to abandon the contract even if it turned out to be well in-the-money.

Well, a strange thing happened with one major client. The client found that its substantial tender-to-contract policy was unfavourable. It studied the documentation. As with most export orders, the exact specification of the order had changed very slightly since the inception of the bidding process and the contracting with the bank. The client claimed that the contract won was not the same as that specified under the tender-to-contract policy, and therefore it was not obliged to enter into the forward contract. The bank was rightly not amused. Was this ethical on the part of the corporate client? Far from it in my opinion.

Rings

Some time ago a minor futures exchange launched a futures contract in an illiquid and not easily observed index. However the market struggled to gain volume. In an attempt to demonstrate activity a prohibited circular trading 'ring' was set up. Apparently certain traders traded with each other to boost the volume of the market and thereby tempt genuine hedgers into the market. Soon after the scandal broke, not only did the particular futures contract stop trading but the futures exchange itself went out of business.

The lessons here are two-fold. Beware of surprisingly active futures markets. Secondly, exchange traded futures, and to a slightly lesser extent derivatives in general, should be based on a recognizably liquid index or commodity with fully transparent and frequently observable prices. These conditions do not appear to be present in the credit derivatives market.

UK local authorities

The Hammersmith & Fulham case (*Hazell v Hammersmith and Fulham London Borough Council*, House of Lords, 1991, 2 WLR P372) has been mentioned in Chapter 10 and elsewhere in this book. In the late 1980s UK municipalities entered into derivatives with banks which were subsequently declared unauthorized or *ultra vires*.

The precise motivation behind the local authorities' operations in these derivatives market is unclear. But it is common knowledge that UK local authorities in the late 1980s were set strict external financing controls by Margaret Thatcher's Conservative government. Opposition Labour party controlled local authorities sought to raise income to fund their spending objectives. Several financial engineering schemes were employed to raise funds whilst meeting the letter of the law. Many local authorities sold options on interest rates in the form of interest rate caps and swaptions to banks. These operations generated cash in the form of premium income. The schemes proved extremely popular amongst several local treasurers and their banks and premiums soon fell to levels well below the market. But interest rates rose and the local authorities were called on to meet their obligations under the interest insurance policies sold. Some local authorities sought to extricate themselves from these liabilities and the episode culminated in the structures being declared *ultra vires*. Local authorities were deemed not to have had the authority to enter into such transactions.

> *'Beware of surprisingly active futures markets.'*

Banks, who had believed that they had been dealing with an arm of the UK Government and thus with entities with an implied AAA rating, were taught a salutary lesson. There was no default. But the legal validity of the transactions was not checked, or if it was, a business risk was taken in view of the large profits to be made. The most successful of the banks were those that took on the initial deals and then sold their positions on to other banks.

As in so many such cases, would the derivatives trading have been declared *ultra vires* if interest rates had fallen and the local authorities had made money? Unlikely, I believe. The time to closely examine financial engineering practices is when they are successful. Any highly profitable trading business should be dissected, understood and explainable. Why is the large profit available? Is there a tax angle? If somebody is being misled, what are the chances that the counterparty will complain? Can you pass the deal off to some other bank whilst top-slicing the profit? What are the due-diligence liabilities, if any, of a broker who passes on the deal? It is also interesting to note that the vast majority of local authorities had not indulged in balance sheet windowdressing and had used swaps for perfectly legitimate hedging purposes. But their swaps too were deemed *ultra vires*.

Banks must tread carefully when assisting with regulatory arbitrage.

BCCI

Around the same time as the local authority swap disaster, the Bank of Credit and Commerce International was closed down for a number of reasons. I do not know if there were any market losses due to derivatives they held, but some municipalities suffered as a result of money market deposits held with BCCI. The local authority had used a broker to place its funds with any bank on the Bank of England list of authorized banks at the highest rates available. The rates being offered by BCCI just before it was closed by the Bank of England were amongst the highest for banks in London. Many banks had had suspicions for some time about the operations of the bank. The broker was mandated to obtain the highest rates possible for the local authority from the list and business drifted to BCCI.

Although the case had nothing to do with new financial instruments, there is a moral to be learned here. As was the case with local authority swaps, management accounting and performance objectives can often lead to the closing of risky trades. In this case there was no performance bonus involved so not a hint of greed dominating money market operations. But there is always a clear and present danger that business moves to the highest return and often higher than acceptable risks. Dealing objectives and mandates should be drawn up carefully.

Orange County

The case of the treasurer of Orange County, Robert Citron, has been mentioned earlier. The voters of Orange County in California were rich but parsimonious. For many years he had won voters' support because of his profitable investments which led to low local taxes. Few questions were asked. But he came under increasing pressure to increase returns and lower taxes still further. His ability to deal in derivatives directly was restricted, but he bought bonds that had currency derivatives embedded within them. Many of the bonds were highly rated and issued by quasi-government mortgage bodies. Orange County suffered its losses not because its treasurer had done anything illegal. After years of making profits for the taxpayers, he claimed ignorance of the true nature of the bonds that he had bought. '*Due to my inexperience I placed a great deal of reliance on the advice of market professionals . . . I wish I had more training in complex government securities,*' he said. The reasons behind apparent outstanding performance should always be examined carefully.

Bankers Trust

Perhaps Bankers Trust began its route into the Deutsche Bank Group as a result of its loss of reputation, following sales of highly structured derivatives to Procter & Gamble and Gibson Greeting in 1994. Both cases were settled out of court. Fairly or unfairly, the rights and wrongs of Bankers Trust's actions in selling the swaps which were highly profitable to them are irrelevant. They were labelled as 'sharp' operators and it would take a brave treasurer to do business with them. If problems ensued, then it would be easy for a board of directors to point to these cases and question why he had dealt with BT. The upside for dealing with BT with other people's money was limited.

It may be argued that the treasurer of an eminent corporation should have been qualified to analyze the swaps that he had bought from Bankers Trust. And perhaps his firm was contractually precluded from showing the deals to others or felt it to be unethical to obtain independent advice from a consultant. But they were not compelled to buy the structures. The case shows that even the appearance of being 'sharp' can leave a permanent scar on a bank.

Nick Leeson at Barings

There are six great powers in Europe: England, France, Prussia, Austria, Russia and Baring Brothers.

DUC DE RICHELIEU

It was the 1980s and traders were young. It was a classic rags-to-riches tale. Leeson was the working class son of a plasterer from Watford, Hertfordshire, who failed his final maths exam and left school with few qualifications.

Leeson got a job as a clerk with royal bank Coutts, followed by a series of jobs with other banks, ending up with Barings Bank. He quickly made a favourable impression and was promoted to the trading floor. Soon Leeson, aged only 26, was appointed manager of futures markets trading on the Singapore Monetary Exchange. The whizz-kid was trusted by his superiors in London, who were delighted with his Midas touch. By 1993, he had generated profits of more than USD10 million – about 10 per cent of Barings Bank's total profit that year. Leeson's team traded large sums and as team leader, controlled the office book-keeping. However in 1994, a mistake by a junior team member started the chain of spiralling losses. A loss of USD20,000 was covered up in an 'error account', 88888, of which London was apparently unaware.

The markets turned against Leeson, accelerated by the economic aftershocks of the Kobe earthquake. But losses were invisible in this 'error' account, so that his trading team in Singapore would always appear in profit.

As the losses grew, Leeson requested extra funds from the head office treasury to make margin calls on his futures losses to continue trading. He hoped to generate profits to cover his losses. In February 1995, Baring's uncovered USD850 million losses. Barings, the UK's oldest merchant bank, finally crashed, and was bought for GBP1 by the Dutch banking and insurance group ING. Executives who were implicated in the failure to control Leeson resigned or were sacked.

'The sign of a well-managed bank is when it carries out a thorough investigation when large profits are made.'

In his autobiography *Rogue Trader*, Leeson said the ethos at Barings was simple: 'We were all driven to make profits, profits, and more profits . . . I was the rising star.' He earned a bonus of GBP130,000 on his salary of GBP50,000.

What seems strange is that Barings was brought down through futures trading and not through any complicated highly structured financial instrument that was difficult to value. In futures markets losses and gains are settled every day as the contracts are re-valued at market. Barings fell not because of Leeson's losses. The bank started on the slippery slope to disaster when it accepted his methods when he was making profits. A telling comment by a senior Barings executive when he disappeared was, 'one of our barrow-boys has gone missing'. The sign of a well-managed bank is when it carries out a thorough investigation when large profits are made. It is rather belated to investigate unexpected losses.

Joseph Jett at Kidder Peabody

Joseph Jett did not steal any money. He did not indulge in any false accounting. He did not misrepresent any trades. Yet, Joseph Jett was, in my opinion, unfairly penalized by Kidder Peabody management for the management accounting system devised by them and not him.

In April 1994, he was fired by Kidder. They accused him, one of Wall Street's most highly successful bond traders, of faking profits to boost his multi-million dollar bonus. Jett has never faced any criminal charges and his frozen bonuses were released. A Securities and Exchange Commission judge cleared him of fraud, but fined him for book-keeping and record-keeping irregularities. Jett appealed against the ruling.

By Jett's own account, he engaged in forward trading of bonds which involved booking profits before they had been realized – a common practice in many trading books. Jett claimed, and tape recordings seem to corroborate this, that his managers at Kidder were fully aware of what he was doing. So was Jett a lone, rogue trader independently exploiting loopholes to produce ghost profits and then systematically covering over his tracks? Whatever the improprieties of his actions, there was little attempt at secrecy or concealment. And Jett still claims that his trades were profitable.

Without first-hand knowledge of the details, I can somehow believe him. In the early 1980s my firm's performance management system monitoring my profitability left a great deal to be desired, though it did not directly generate bonuses. My US dollar borrowing on behalf of the firm was measured against US dollar LIBOR. My US dollar investments, on the other hand, were measured against the interest rate paid on the firm's call account, some 1.5 per cent below LIBOR. Beating the flat LIBOR borrowing benchmark was pretty difficult to achieve on a regular basis in the money markets, but achieving a deposit rate higher than the benchmark set was no problem. Now sterling investments and borrowing were somebody else's problem. If I was paid strictly on profits generated, I would have been tempted to eliminate any US dollar borrowings through USD/GBP foreign exchange swaps. I could have bought US dollars spot and simultaneously sold US dollars forward for a week or a month. And that would have almost magically converted my US dollar borrowing position into a US dollar investment position. Instead of losing against my management accounting benchmark by more than 0.125 per cent, I would have easily beaten the deposit benchmark by nearly 1.375 per cent and often more.

Jett was accused of booking unrealized profits. Many investment or loan portfolios do just the opposite. They do not mark positions to market. Future losses would be the concern of future desk managers. Such supervisory practices have led to the creation of well-above-LIBOR-yielding products, with a compensating degrading in value perhaps through embedded options sold to the issuer.

Market squeezing

Canada's *Financial Post* reported, on 12 May 1999, that Credit Suisse First Boston was fined by the Stockholm Stock Exchange for attempted stock market manipulation. 'The two million kroner (USD348,000) fine imposed on CSFB related to attempted manipulation of a share index by the three British.' Mats Wilhelmsson, the Stockholm Stock Exchange's head of market surveillance, said: 'Mr Archer (a CSFB trader) tried to manipulate share prices of what was one of the oldest companies in the world, Stora.' According to the *Financial Times* of 12 May 1999, 'The CSFB traders hatched and embarked on a series of fictitious transactions in Stora shares in an effort to manipulate Stockholm's OMX index and generate a profit of about USD700,000.' Such cash market manipulation is relatively easy to effect in illiquid emerging stockmarkets.

I have seen fairly small purchases in the Korean stockmarket make disproportionate changes in the KOSPI, the Korean stockmarket index. Even in the UK in the early 1990s there appeared to be systematic movements of GBP three-month LIBOR just before the fixing of the LIFFE short sterling interest rate contract. A number of traders who specialized in arbitraging the futures contracts against the FRA contracts found that their expected profitable positions rapidly turned sour. It is all very well having sophisticated PhD-generated mathematical models to indicate strategies, but when the time comes to collect, the market can completely change character and produce a nasty surprise.

'It is all very well having sophisticated PhD-generated mathematical models to indicate strategies, but when the time comes to collect, the market can completely change character and produce a nasty surprise.'

Such market squeezing was also featured in the Sumitomo copper scandal which came to light in June 1996. Yasuo Hamanaka succeeded in losing USD2.6 billion for Sumitomo. According to the *Guardian* of 4 June 1999: 'Sumitomo is thought to be planning further writs against institutions it believes provided financial and other help to Hamanaka in his three-year reign as king of the copper market in the mid-1990s. Without clearance from his superiors at Sumitomo, the trader cornered huge amounts of metal in what US regulators have described as "one of the most serious world-wide manipulations of a commodities market in 25 years".' Hamanaka was an unusual case in that his personal bonus was not directly linked to his profits and he acted out of self pride.

Loan-linked derivatives

Principle. A thing which too many people confound with interest.

AMBROSE BIERCE

I have come across a surprisingly large number of instances in leveraged buy-out (LBO) and a management buy-out (MBO) financing where the lead banks in the loan syndicate insist on providing interest rate hedging to the borrowers. At first this sounds very altruistic. And of course it is in the lending banks' interests that the borrowers maintain their ability to pay interest on the loan. A sharp rise in interest rates could jeopardize such an ability and has been known to push fledgling companies into liquidation.

So what's the catch? The sting is that the providers of the interest rate insurance obtain a monopoly on selling caps or swaps with no control on pricing other than their conscience. So beware of entering into sole provider agreements with no control over pricing.

US-64

There are many unit trusts that provide guaranteed minimum returns on equity-linked investments. These funds obtain equity market index options or use part of the capital raised to buy zero coupon bonds, thereby ensuring a minimum value to an investor. But there are not many successful funds that can provide a guaranteed dividend of 20 per cent.

India's biggest mutual fund, the government controlled US-64, got into difficulties in September 1998. The USD5 billion fund found itself with a shortfall of USD1 billion between its assets and liabilities, largely because of its practice of providing assured returns to market-based net asset value pricing over a three-year period. The *Financial Times* of 19 March 1999 quoted a member of the committee that issue the rescue plan: 'You cannot have a scheme which invests in equity and gives a guarantee of 20 per cent. It is absurd.'

If you invest in a fund with a guarantee ensure that it is realistic, and that the managers have taken steps to manage or re-insure that risk.

Guaranteed annuity policies

In Chapter 9, 'Hedge choice and performance measurement', I related how UK annuity providers had provided guaranteed minimum annuity rates in the late 1980s. But they largely and collectively ignored the interest rate risk in the belief that interest rates would never fall to the rates implied by the guaranteed annuities.

One of the insurance companies with the guaranteed annuity problem, the Equitable Life Assurance Society, instigated a test case in July 1999 to obtain a court ruling on its actions. The Equitable, a mutual life assurer and incidentally the world's oldest assurance company, had decided that since they were likely to be called to meet the guarantees on their annuity rates, they were going to include the bonus element as part of the guaranteed annuity rates. They declared that if they paid the guaranteed rates plus the bonuses, other members of the mutual would suffer. Quite true but irrelevant. The Equitable won the case, but it is under appeal at the time of writing. Why did they not manage the interest rate risk either by altering the duration of their investments in fixed-rate government securities or by re-insuring?

Again, be careful when providing commitments and beware of commitments lightly given. Ensure that your clients understand the commitments.

Buy back

For the avoidance of doubt, I wish to clearly state that I know of no malpractice or mis-representation in the case below. I am including it here to illustrate a pitfall for an investor that in this case appears at face value to have been adequately handled.

In May 1999 Formula One Administration, the promoter of Grand Prix racing issued bonds secured by the income on television rights. On 30 June 1999, the *Financial Times* revealed that the 'European Commission had concluded that the TV contracts against which the bonds were issued might have to be renegotiated to comply with European law'. The investment banks that led the issue, Morgan Stanley Dean Witter and West LB, indicated that they were prepared to buy back the bonds from investors con-cerned about the legality of the television contracts, even though there was no obliga-tion on the part of the lead banks to buy back the issue. The position of the banks that originally sold the issue was not a legal one, but one of managing their reputa-tion and protecting future business. No investor would

> *'A general buy-back offer, even when written into the documentation, is worthless unless there are clear terms attached, such as a minimum price or declared and reasonable bid–offer price spread.'*

buy another bond from a bank that washed its hands of a bond issue that ran into difficulties.

However a buy-back guarantee is of little real benefit to investors, and investors in instruments with such guarantees should not be lulled into a false sense of comfort. A general buy-back offer, even when written into the documentation, is worthless unless there are clear terms attached, such as a minimum price or declared and reasonable bid–offer price spread.

Conclusion

Beware of trades and commissions that appear to be just too good to be true. They are so often just that. Beware of traders keeping too tight a control over information. But that said, genuine infor-mation must be paid for. So often a creative deal presented by a bank to a client is then presented around the market by the client for a better price. It is seldom difficult to price a transaction or to solve a problem. The difficulty is in identifying a problem. It is unethical for a corporation to disclose a proprietary structure with-out permission. After all, the client is under no obligation to enter into the structure with the originating bank.

I recall a highly structured swap marketed by a bank. The bank selling the swap was prepared to do the deal for a margin of 5 basis points per annum. Intense negotiations were pursued for several months. Eventually the bank would agree to a fee of 4.25 basis points per annum. But behind the scenes the bank was making a huge profit of 40 basis points.

But is making a large profit unethical? If the counterparty was another bank or financial institution or indeed a major corporation, then they should have had sufficient analytical power at their command to protect their own interests. Of course a bank providing an advisory service has a duty of care to its client. But just because someone is making a huge profit out of a deal with you does not mean that you are making a loss. You may have been making an opportunity loss, but the deal could have been good for you in terms of protecting your interests or eliminating your exposure to a certain kind of risk.

Markets are far from perfect. The key to innovation is to create a composite product that adds value to a transaction benefiting both buyer and seller. But too often when a bank talks about a 'needs-driven customer service', the needs referred to are those of its bonus-driven traders seeking new Ferraris. It is just that their needs are deemed to be greater than those of their clients.

In my opinion, one recent financial disaster may not have been a disaster at all, but it turned into one. Metallgesellschaft apparently lost money when hedging long-term oil contracts using short-term oil futures contracts. There are indications that the original 'losses' were largely accounting losses. But when management took firm action in closing the books in the face of adverse publicity, real losses materialized as the markets anticipated the unwinding of the positions and moved against Metallgesellschaft. Sometimes life does imitate the art of many management accounting systems.

As the internet spreads to the financial markets, the credibility implied by a professional-looking Website and a dot.com address may well trap the unwary. If the firm's virtual presence does not match its supposed physical presence, keep away. My e-mail in-box receives dozens of 'hard-to-resist' offers of bonds and stock every week. No doubt some are genuine but I'm sure some are as ephemeral as the 1866 issue of Port of Cordova, Argentina, bonds described by Ken Follett in his book *Dangerous Fortune*.

And finally . . .

The few cases illustrated here show that the majority of losses have had nothing to do with derivatives or new financial instruments. Some have resulted from just plain old-fashioned greed and a lack of control. And imprecise management accounting schemes used to pay personal 'performance' linked bonuses can easily be used to generate profits by any trader worth his place in the trading room. There is insufficient cross-checking, and bosses can be lulled into taking a lenient approach when their own income is correlated with the performance of their staff. Finally, always remember that free lunches are very hard to find. If you don't understand the reasons behind that extra special deal, keep away from it. It could be a gamble or a rip-off.

Everything has been thought of before, but the problem is to think of it again.

_____

GOETHE

CHAPTER

14

The financial future

Likely developments

So what kind of products can we see in the future? One thing certain is that we will see a return to simplicity and some genuine innovations.

Markets demonstrate collective amnesia all too often and reinvent products on a regular basis. As clients get more and more sophisticated and, arguably more importantly, as the tax authorities and regulators keep up with the innovators in the market, there will be a move to genuine-need products that fulfil a real demand, rather than the bank salesman's need to generate a bonus.

Reports of the demise of plain vanilla foreign exchange trading have been greatly exaggerated. With the creation of the euro, the trading that took place between the D-mark bloc and the Mediterranean bloc will be replaced by convergence trading between the euro and other EU currencies and the euro and East European currencies. Furthermore, the Asian currency crises in 1997/98 showed that emerging markets are not just one pool. The differing impact the crises had on the various 'emerging' markets showed that these markets are quite different. What holds them together is the fund manager's risk-aversion and his trustee's 20/20 vision. No manager wants to be caught doing something that nobody else is doing. In turbulent times, the manager of other people's money runs for cover. There is a flight to quality which spells bad news for all emerging markets.

This same instinct applies to products and banks. If a certain kind of product has led to a large loss in an organization, then treasurers will think twice before exposing themselves to criticism, even if they themselves understand the product and are confident in its applicability to their organizations.

In terms of genuine innovations, we will continue to see credit derivatives grow. But are these new products, or are they just variations on credit insurance and asset swaps which have been around for decades?

Insurance derivatives will also continue to grow. But surely option-related derivatives products are one kind of insurance product or other? They have always been explained to end-users as financial insurance. The trouble was that they could not be called 'insurance products' because insurance in most countries has been the preserve of insurance companies, and banks have been prohibited from entering this area.

'In turbulent times, the manager of other people's money runs for cover.'

In the same way, insurance companies have not for some time been providers of insurance. They have been in the savings business. And banks have been in the insurance business through their derivatives and new issue underwriting businesses. I see the differences in regulation between banks and insurance companies disappearing completely early in the millennium. There will just be wholesale financial companies and retail financial companies.

Less technophilia – have faith in fools

The models tell you where things will be in five years. But they don't tell you what happens before you get to the moment of certainty.

AYMAN HINDY,

strategist, Long Term Capital Management

Perhaps the treasury management pendulum has swung too far in the direction of technophilia and away from common sense. Value @ Risk and other measures have become the be-all-and-end-all of risk management. The assumptions behind Nobel Prize winners' models are infrequently questioned. But it is not a question of barrow-boy uneducated trader versus physics PhD. It is just that the balance has swung too far towards blind faith in calculations that boards do not adequately understand, and more dangerously, are too embarrassed to demand justification. It is incredible that the entire case by Kidder Peabody against Joseph Jett was that he used the management accounting system designed by *them* to generate performance bonuses. There should be more emphasis on the big picture. Bank and corporate boards should hire more fools. The fools should have a brief to question everything. If only Korean banks had had a few fools to question loans to *chaebols* . . .

Dealers can outwit accountants

Derivatives provide finance directors with very useful tools for managing risk or for providing clients with an enhanced service; because they are off-balance sheet and don't require a significant cash outlay (if at all) they can quickly spell big trouble.

Every dealer worth hiring is capable of manipulating his profit and loss account to a desired level. Management accounting reports seldom accurately reflect the risk on a portfolio of complex financial instruments. Good dealers can outwit their internal or external auditors. Moreover, individual performance bonuses can encourage at best 'accounting engineering', a 'double-or-quit' attitude or outright fraud. Dealers have a free option. Employers don't sue them for losses. Bonuses should be based on team performance – conspiracies seldom hold firm for long. Ensure sound character of Treasury staff. This is just as important as technical ability and ensures that Treasury performance targets are realistic.

Technological over-confidence

---

21 August 1998 was the worst day in the young history of scientific finance. On that day alone, Long Term Capital lost USD550 million.

MICHAEL LEWIS.

Extract from 'How the Eggheads Cracked', *New York Times*, 24 January 1999

Ever sophisticated technology on its own is no solution. It has to be correctly interpreted. And the limitations of the information and output must be understood.

On the morning of 7 December 1941 the very latest technological device alerted its operator. The place was Pearl Harbor, Hawaii and the device was the Westinghouse long-range radar. The machine detected a squadron of planes approaching, but the officer assumed that the planes were American B-17s. The rest is history.

Similar human error and over-confidence in technology was the cause of the bombing of the Chinese embassy in Belgrade on 7 May 1999. Three days before Nato bombed the embassy, a military intelligence officer told colleagues that the wrong building had been chosen. The intelligence analyst noticed surveillance photographs of the building proposed for a Nato strike did not appear to coincide with the intended target, the Yugoslav Federal Directorate of Supply and Procurement (FDSP). The analyst did not know that the building in question was in fact the Chinese embassy. Apparently, a series of errors caused the bombing. First, CIA staff were using old maps and databases which did not show that the embassy had moved location. Then an analyst made a mistaken assumption about the FDSP's location based on its address. Finally, a second analyst noticed discrepancies between the FDSP's supposed location and that of the target building. This middle-ranking

> *'Probabilistic models have to be understood for what they are.'*

officer called another middle-ranking officer in Europe and conveyed his concerns, and at the same time he tried to fix a meeting within the CIA to relay his concerns. But he failed to arrange the meeting at the CIA. He then went off for scheduled training, and when he returned on 7 May he found that the raid was planned for that night. According to *The Washington Post* he was told: *'The bombers are in the air. It's too late.'*

Such a mix-up can happen in war. It can also occur in technologically dependent financial management. Technology-generated risk management outputs have to be correctly interpreted in a very short time. And the assumptions behind complex derivative models and inputs must be carefully examined and agreed to by controllers and management. And the outputs should be examined with a certain degree of cynicism. Have conditions in the markets changed since the models were developed? Have the models been adapted from a completely different market? The models may work very well in the US or the UK, but do they apply in an illiquid emerging market? If your dealers cannot explain a third-generation derivative to you in simple terms, and, in turn, you cannot demystify the products in front of shareholders at an Annual General Meeting, ask yourself the questions:

- Is it appropriate to this business?
- Do we really need to do it?

If the answers are Yes and Yes, make sure you understand it.

Probabilistic models have to be understood for what they are. I remember hearing at maths class at high school. 'A man can drown in a lake three feet deep *on average*.' There is now empirical evidence to this effect. In September 1997 in Detroit, a 41-year-old man got stuck and drowned in two feet of water. He had squeezed headfirst through an 18-inch-wide sewer grate to retrieve his car keys.

Trading decisions nevertheless have to be made. There is a risk associated with every decision. Some years ago the head of Human Resources at a US bank in London had a really bright idea for hiring new staff. The HR head observed that the bank's dealers spent all day in front of computer monitors. *'Who else does that?'* he wondered. The bank hired several bright air traffic controllers as dealers. They very soon picked up the technicalities of foreign exchange spot and forward. But as proficient air traffic controllers they had been trained to avoid risk at all costs. They just sat in front of their screens neither buying nor selling.

Mathematical ability and familiarity with computer screens is not enough to make a good dealer. According to a study by Elizabeth Brannon and Herbert Terrace of Columbia University, published in the journal, *Science*, November 1998, even monkeys can grasp the concept of numbers. Two rhesus monkeys named Rosencrantz and Macduff were taught to count using touch-sensitive computer screens of images that each contained from one to four objects. First, the monkeys were taught to touch the screens in order, from the image with one object to the image with four objects. 'A monkey learns by trial and error,' said Brannon, a graduate student. If the monkey touched all four pictures in the right order, he got a banana treat. If the monkey made an error, the screen blacked out.

The rhesus monkeys were more than happy to make mathematical decisions and make errors in the pursuit of banana-flavoured pellets. And the air-traffic controllers just would not trade.

Liquidity and chaos

A cynic is a man who knows the price of everything, and the value of nothing.

OSCAR WILDE

In December 1997, the International Monetary Fund criticized Korean banks for relying on short-term foreign loans 'leaving the nation vulnerable to a liquidity crisis'. So true. As I wrote in the *Financial Times* of 5 December 1997, 'Continental Illinois and so many other cases have shown that contrary to the text-book view, efficient liquidity management is not about holding a certain percentage of government bonds. It is about diversifying liabilities. Rather than get fixated over macho exotic options, bankers the world over should study history.'

Many young investment bankers are highly proficient at pricing anything and everything. They can price any financial instrument, strip away a conversion option from a fixed-interest component and then combine it with another structure in a third currency. But markets often just don't play according to the rules. Continental Illinois and even the expertly run Long Term Capital Management found that in their hour of need the realization value of their sophistically priced investments was nowhere near their theoretical value. These 'pricers' who know the price of everything religiously believe that everything has a price implied through received math ematical formulae, independent of market value. And then risk managers are led to believe their own theoretical valuations and use these derived prices to manage risk. But the valuation of a security is only really necessary and therefore meaningful in times of chaos. And in times of chaos conventional models just do not work.

Chaos theory was first discovered perhaps by a meteorologist named Edward Lorenz. In 1961, working on a weather forecasting model, he had a computer set up, with a set of 12 equations. He identified a particular pattern which he wanted to see again. To save time – and remember this was way before the advent of Pentium IIIs – he started in the middle of the sequence, instead of the beginning. He entered the reading at the halfway stage from the earlier series and left the computer to churn out the series again.

When Lorenz returned an hour later, the sequence generated proved quite different. Instead of being identical to the previous pattern, the new series ended very differently from the original. He eventually worked out what had occurred. His computer's memory stored the numbers to six decimal places. But to economize on paper, he only had it print out the results to three decimal places. In the original sequence, the true number at the halfway point was .506127. But the output stored was only to the first three decimals showing .506. It was this truncated number that was input as the starting point for the second computer run.

> *'A healthy dose of scepticism is needed for survival.'*

Lorenz proved that a small difference could make a huge discrepancy in outcome. This effect came to be known as the 'butterfly effect'.

> The flapping of a single butterfly's wing today produces a tiny change in the state of the atmosphere. Over a period of time, what the atmosphere actually does diverges from what it would have done. So, in a month's time, a tornado that would have devastated the Indonesian coast doesn't happen. Or maybe one that wasn't going to happen, does. (Ian Stewart, *Does God Play Dice? The Mathematics of Chaos*)

Nick Leeson just before his fall was supposed to be arbitraging tiny differences between Japanese stockmarket Nikkei indices quoted in the Tokyo and Singapore futures exchanges. The Kobe earthquake put paid to his strategy and he ended in jail. Long Term Capital Management's 'hedge fund' suffered because of the crisis in Russian financial markets, which resulted from the East Asian crisis.

Believing one's own models is a certain recipe for disaster. A healthy dose of scepticism is needed for survival.

The evil that men do lives after them

Shakespeare pointed out a common directors' dilemma: whilst errors of judgement stand out to be criticized in hindsight, 'the good lies interred with their bones' – although it seems unlikely that a derivatives dealer will meet the fate of Julius Caesar. However, we can recall with some irony the voters' support for Orange County's Treasury in the days when it was making money and lowering taxes; and consider that Barings' board was taking its full share of the jailed Mr Leeson's profit before his fall. Would Nick Leeson have been jailed if he had continued to make money for his masters? In my opinion, not very likely! But such are the inevitable perils of managing other people's money! Plenty of friends in times of plenty, but handwashing when losses arise.

Few boards understood what treasurers were doing

A derivative is like a razor. You can use it to shave yourself and make yourself attractive to your girlfriend. You can slit her throat with it. Or you can use it to commit suicide.

ANON

Finally, it is incumbent on the boards of directors to understand and use appropriate derivatives. Shareholders have successfully sued when they have not been used. They might eventually get very annoyed if they are misused. The *Financial Times'* Lex column of 9 March 1995 said: *'The retreat by industrial companies is also sensible, given that few boards really understood what their corporate treasurers were doing. But derivatives are still valuable tools if used to hedge risks rather than speculate. The longer-term answer is for boards to do their homework rather than to impose a ban.'*

But the lessons learned from the demise of the so-called 'hedge fund' Long Term Capital Management, a firm managed by Wall Street's 'masters of the universe' suggests that it is not just corporate boards of directors that need to do their homework. How many senior bankers or regulators really understand the risks that banks or their clients are carrying on their books? There is a touching blind faith in the computer outputs produced by the rocket science mathematical modelling of financial derivatives. And this extends down to the use of financial calculators, which I forbid in my training programmes. Most financial calculations can be effected on a simple high school scientific calculator. And know the answer before running your computer program. Commonsense 'foolish' guesstimates are not always made.

I was recently asked by a client bank to analyze a complex structured cross-currency swap with embedded third-currency and term options. An investment bank offered my client USD0.3 million to close out the transaction. Without any mechanical aids, I guessed a figure of USD6 million. Using a scientific calculator I produced a valuation of USD6.55 million. Developing and testing a computer simulation model, I refined the answer to USD6.42 million. No high technology was needed to realize that my client's investment bank was attempting 'ignorance arbitrage'.

Innovation by banks in new financial instruments is necessary as it is in any industry to avoid being left behind in the competitive marketplace. And there will be a number of genuinely useful products that meet customers' needs. These needs may be fiscal or regulatory; or the packaged return or cost of a bond issue or loan plus a structured swap may be more favourable; or because they have been engineered to generate a specifically required exposure; or because they neatly hedge an asset or liability exposure. But if the bank selling the products or corporation buying these instruments does not understand why they are entering into such transactions and how to measure and control the risks generated by them, it would be better to steer well clear of them.

Let us be thankful for the fools. But for them the rest of us could not succeed.

MARK TWAIN

And finally . . .

Ralph, my father-in-law's dog, was included in my dedications at the beginning of this book. Let me update an old story:

I heard that in view of the emerging markets financial crisis the dealing room of a major bank is being downsized. There will be a total crew of three: a computer, a man, and a dog. *'What? Is the dog going to be dealing?'* I asked. *'Don't be a fool,'* I was told. *'The dog is the back office. He is there to make sure nobody touches the computer'*. *'And the man?'* I asked. *'Stupid question. He is the middle office. His job is to feed the dog.'* Corporate and bank presidents should follow the example set by mediaeval kings and emperors. They would do well to hire a few fools to ask stupid questions.

VI

Appendices

The appendices are very much an integral part of the body of this book. May I suggest that even readers with a severe form of *appendicitis librarius* should avoid performing an appendectomy on this book.

Derivatives were first constructed as a means of hedging risk. In fact they were known as hedging or risk management products developed before the 'D' word was coined in the mid-1980s. It is natural, therefore, for me to include as Appendix 1, a list of 'Financial risk types' in the first section of Part VI. Appendix 2 is a list of 'Financial risk management instruments'. The list is not simply a dry shopping-list of financial products. It is an opinionated commentary with words of warning on these key instruments.

This is not just a book about derivatives. The key financial instruments described here include innovative cash instruments that may or may not have required derivatives in their construction. Appendix 3 is a glossary of 'Risk management terms' used elsewhere in the book or in the markets.

Finally, in Appendix 4, I have included a detailed look at Islamic financial products. Even if you are not particularly interested in such products may I suggest that you should be. The thought and management processes required in Islamic financial instrument innovation can be used in the innovation process applied in any other financial market that seeks to take advantage of, comply with or avoid external rules and regulations or costs.

Appendix 1: Financial risk types or '50 ways to lose your money'

The title of this Appendix paraphrases the Paul Simon song. Incidentally, '50 ways to lose your lover' was written in 1975 when I first carried out research into the term structure of interest rates, an essential tool in the development of derivatives.

To put it simply and directly, if the bosses do not or cannot understand both the risks and rewards in their products, their firm should not be in the business.

WILLIAM J. MCDONOUGH,
President, Federal Reserve Bank of New York

Acquisition risk

Do you really know what you are buying? Even if the price to be paid to the receivers is a nominal GBP1 as was the case with Barings, what is the true value of the assets and liabilities of the firm that you are buying? In some countries, bank accounting is highly creative. On the other hand, as the target of acquisitive companies, are you spending too much management time fending off predators?

Careless error risk

Overconfidence leads to errors. I still vividly remember as a raw but cocksure dealer nearly 20 years ago, saying, *'Buy dollars'* when I meant, *'Buy pounds'*. It was highly embarrassing but it was quickly sorted out. Fix the problem immediately.

Commodity risk

Are your customers subject to gold or other commodity prices? Gold or copper producers could have their borrowing liabilities linked to the gold price. See *Energy price risk*.

Communication risk

Send that confirmation now! See *Language risk*. And avoid jargon. Don't talk about 'strangles' and 'straddles'. What is really going on in the deal? Tell it like it is.

Competence/understanding

If you don't understand your dealers, don't let them do it! Don't be afraid of your own ignorance. Go on a course – or buy a book. Don't be afraid to ask seemingly stupid questions. See *Fraud (staff) risk*.

Competitive risk

Don't put off that product too long even if it is going to compete with existing products. Somebody else will build a better mortgage product if you do not. Like Virgin Direct! Don't rely on superior current market share. Be innovative or ready to immediately react to competitors.

Concentration of assets risk

Large exposure risk is obvious and there are central bank limits in most (but not all) countries. Sometimes governments direct banks to lend to certain champion industries. Later, of course, they have to call the International Monetary Fund!

Concentration of business-type risk

With the merger of Citicorp and Travelers into Citigroup it seems that financial supermarkets are again the fashion. On the other hand, Barclays Capital says in its advertisements, 'Stick to your strengths'. But if the market moves and regulations change, can you re-invent your institution?

Concentration of liabilities risk

Diversify your liabilities. Retail bankers have fewer liquidity problems than wholesale bankers do. Do not place yourself at the mercy of a few lenders. See *Liquidity risk*.

Convertibility risk

Also known as 'deliverability risk'. Can the currency be converted and delivered into a freely tradable currency? Non-deliverable forwards are widely used in Asia and in Eastern Europe partly in an attempt to neutralize this type of risk.

Country risk

Do you really understand what is happening in Indonesia or Korea? Can you control your Asian subsidiary from afar without offending everyone? Or your aggressive Californian subsidiary or branch without killing motivation?

Credit risk

So how much has the customer borrowed elsewhere? Has your client used off-balance sheet finance excessively? Will the parent or government really stand by that bank? You could buy these new fashionable credit derivatives. But see *Legal risk*. Know your customer. Not just the firm but the human being you are dealing with.

Cultural risk

'My word is my bond' is the rule in London. But be warned. It does not apply everywhere, even after contracts have been exchanged! Contracts are sometimes seen as a basis for negotiation. See also *Fraud (customer) risk*.

Currency economic risk

Japanese producers faced severe competition from Korean producers post the devaluation of the Korean won. The Japanese suffered from economic exposure with respect to the won. Few corporate treasurers hedge economic exposure.

Currency transaction risk

This is the risk that foreign currency receivables will change in home currency terms. But what is a loss? How are you, as the treasurer, measured? Are you measured against the spot rate outcome? Or against the forward rate at the time the underlying transaction is made? Or against the average exchange rate over the year?

Currency translation risk

It is the risk of revaluation of foreign assets or liabilities as a result of a movement in currency value. No cash flow here. There may be taxation difficulties. Not many corporate treasurers hedge translation exposure.

Customer satisfaction risk

Do your customers like doing business with you? Will they come back for more of the same? Do they call you for other products?

Disaster recovery risk

Are you prepared? If you lose GBP80 million on interest rate caps, what does the market think of you? Be sure to watch carefully traders who are making substantial profits. If they say it is 'arbitrage', make sure it is. Genuine arbitrage is still possible. However, if the profits are speculation generated, they will probably turn into losses! See *Fraud (staff) risk*.

Economic activity risk

A slowdown in economic activity will affect your business. Your overheads have still to be paid for. A downturn in international trade will effect the foreign exchange and financing business of banks.

Energy price risk

Do you have airline customers who could use energy derivatives? Oil producers, such as Mexico, have had the interest rate on their bond liabilities linked to the price of oil. See also *Commodity risk*.

Environment risk

If you lend to polluters, you may be faced with competition from a bank like the Co-operative Bank that does not. See *Image risk*.

Equity market risk

Are you about to launch a rights issue? Use equity derivatives to hedge the issue. But do check regulatory compliance issues to be sure that you cannot be accused of insider trading.

Fraud (banker) risk

Has your banker misrepresented that complex geared swap? Make sure you tape all conversations – learn from Linda Tripp.

Fraud (customer) risk

Will your client say that he did not understand that complex geared swap? All will be fine if the client is 'in the money'. He will only cry 'foul' if things start to go sour for him!

Fraud (staff) risk

This often follows a covered-up disaster. See *Disaster recovery risk*. And watch the traders who don't take holidays. Many an irregularity has surfaced when a trader who never took a holiday fell ill and his position was taken over by a colleague.

Image/PR risk

A recovery from a bout of bad publicity is extremely difficult. See *Disaster recovery risk* and *Fraud (banker) risk*. Keep the media, rating agencies and your counterparties fully informed of any potential difficulties. Prepare a list of questions and answers for your CEO. No fund manager or treasurer wants to hold an asset or do business with a bank that suffers from adverse reporting in the media.

Information risk

Keep your mouth shut and ears open especially in bars in the City of London or Wall Street or in other financial centres. Read the *Financial Times* on the train or the aeroplane. Even a small piece of information may be somebody else's missing link. Not so long ago a train commuter sitting next to me was reading his papers on the way to work. It was headed 'Confidential: "Big" Bank Product

Development Department'. And beware of the boastful. In my experience the most leaky are the most senior.

Inflation risk

Many utilities have inflation-linked price controls. Issuing a bond linked to inflation allows them to provide an investment vehicle to pension funds and other savers who seek to generate inflation-adjusted annuities.

Interaction risk

Also known as 'correlation risk'. Is the Hong Kong dollar or Saudi riyal really fixed to the US dollar? What if monetary union within Europe fails and the Euro collapses?

Interest rate risk

Are you selling fixed-rate mortgages? If you are in the property business, even if you are not financing, you suffer from interest rate risk. Demand for property is linked to interest rates. As a retail banker, your cheque account business will lose profitability as interest rates fall. Overheads are fixed costs.

Language risk

When your customers/subordinates say 'Yes', do they just mean, 'I heard you?' See *Communication risk*. Also be careful about the symbol 'M'. It may mean a million or a thousand!

Legal risk

Were those nice UK Local Authority swap dealers acting *intra vires*? Do you really think that credit derivatives are not insurance contracts and therefore prohibited to banks in most countries?

Liquidity risk

Also known as solvency risk. Liquidity is much less about holding liquid assets than about managing and diversifying liabilities. Remember Continental Illinois! See *Concentration of liabilities risk* and *Image risk*.

Morbidity risk

Are your staff sickly? Alcoholics? Drug users? Don't be too reliant on any one person. Or is someone likely to impact on others' performance through racist or sexist remarks?

Mortality risk

See *Morbidity risk*, but only more so. Copy the Royal Family. Catch separate flights on trips. And don't even think about buying key-man insurance. Just make sure that at least two people can do the job.

Operational risk

This is everything other than market-related risks.

Performance measurement risk

Any dealer worth hiring can manage his management accounts and can show bookkeeping profits at the expense of real losses. Dealing mandates provide only a little more protection than a comfort blanket. See *Fraud (staff) risk*.

Political risk

What will happen if there is a coup in Indonesia? Will the new government abide by the IMF's terms? Will the IRA or ETA bomb your dealing room?

Property (real estate) risk

Do your property asset-backed loans have sufficient cover? Is the property liquid? See also *Interest rate risk*.

Rating agency risk

What if Moody's and S&P downgrade you or your investments? There is evidence that lower rated bonds default more than higher rated bonds. I am reminded, however, of the sick man who refused to go to bed. More people die in bed than in the living room. Other than the financial market equivalent of a car crash (Barings?), corporate mortality is usually associated with firms in deteriorating stages of morbidity.

Regulatory risk

If you operate in several countries you may face inconsistent rules. Some countries insist branches be ringfenced for regulatory capital purposes.

Religious risk

Is interest *Hallal* or *Haram*? Is usury a problem? A particular form of ethical risk. See also *Environment risk* and *Image risk*.

Resignation risk

Will the star dealing team move to a competitor after you buy the bank? Maybe there should be football-style transfer fees in dealing rooms?

Settlement risk

Remember Herstatt? This is the risk that you meet your part of the bargain and your counterparty does not. Herstatt Bank collected

D-mark receipts on foreign exchange contracts but did not fulfil its US dollar payment obligations. There are now netting procedures in place to avoid this problem.

Systemic risk

Financial instability is contagious. Financial systems are closely interlinked. Instability in Indonesia or Korea has a domino effect on Hong Kong, Tokyo and London.

Tax risk

What did you write on that tax-based savings scheme document? In 1997, substantial losses were suffered by equity index option writes. Changes in the treatment of the tax credit associated with UK shares surprised the market just when margins had narrowed through competition.

Technological risk

A missing fax was the cause of recent interbank dispute. A fax was sent exercising an option. It was sent to a fax machine in the bank writing the option, but apparently it was never received by the options desk. I receive several stray faxes for a major law firm every week. Before sending an important fax, check the number; after sending it, confirm receipt.

Other than the millennium bug, there is also the Dow Jones 10,000 scare. Can your systems manage? Can you cope with computer/telephone system failure? Also see *Political risk*. Establish a second dealing room elsewhere.

Transport risk

Remember the crash of 1987? That day there was a severe storm in London. Trees were blown on to railway tracks. Many people were late for work.

Weather risk

See *Environment risk* and *Transport risk*.

It's impossible to take an unnecessary risk. Because you only find out whether a risk was unnecessary after you've taken it.

GIOVANNI AGNELLI,
President, FIAT

No risk

This final risk is the most insidious and dangerous risk. 'No risk' is the risk of having a risk manager who always says 'No', and who comes up with 50 or so ways not to do the business. Of course, you will never appear to lose money. You will never be known for making a wrong decision. It is just that the business will go elsewhere and your firm will find itself with unemployed capital!

Website: www.dc3.co.uk/risks.htm

A derivative is neither a 'gift from God' nor 'a creation of the devil', rather a useful tool in the hands of the informed practitioner. You would not put a chainsaw in the hands of a child, nor should the uninitiated or overtly reckless be let loose on derivatives.

ANNE-MARIA WILFLING-ROTHENSTEIN,
European Head of Sales, Treasury & Capital markets,
KBC Bank, Brussels

Appendix 2: Financial risk management instruments

This list of financial instruments is more than a conventional glossary. It is a self-contained explanation of the derivative products developed in the market and highlights the relationship between them.

Accreting cap

A cap in which the notional principal amount increases over the life of the instrument. The premium is lower than if the writer of the cap were to pay interest differentials on the maximum (final) principal amount.

Accreting swap

A swap in which the notional principal amount increases over the life of the swap. In project finance, the financing requirement is usually scheduled to rise through the life of the project. In other cases drawdown on a facility is staggered by the company in accordance with requirements. An accreting swap allows a company to increase its swap amount on a pre-scheduled basis to match the principal in the underlying borrowing. The notional amount of the swap into fixed-rate financing therefore rises in line with the amount borrowed until the loan is scheduled to be fully utilized.

Amortizing cap

The opposite of an accreting cap. Here the principal amount falls according a pre-determined schedule. The premium is therefore lower than if the writer of the cap were to pay interest differentials on the initial principal amount.

Amortizing swap

The opposite of an accreting swap. It is a swap in which the notional principal decreases over the life of the swap. As with the accreting swap, the amortizing swap allows a company to match the swap to its cash flows. If a company has a sinking fund bond issue or a loan that amortizes, such as in many leasing arrangements, an amortizing swap allows the company to convert its debt from fixed rate to floating rate or *vice versa*.

Asset swap

Swaps were originally developed to aid the restructuring of liabilities. An asset swap involves altering the payment basis on assets. However the terms of the swap are identical to normal interest rate or currency swaps. It is just the purpose that is different. The theory behind asset swaps is that bond investors are more credit sensitive than loan participators. Bank loans are usually at floating rate. If a company is in difficulties, its bond price falls faster than its loan margin rises. Such bonds are bought and swapped into floating rate 'synthetic loan assets' for bank investors using an asset swap to generate a packaged yield over LIBOR greater than in the loan market.

Atlantic option

Also known as an 'Icelandic option'. Somewhat of a cross between a European option and an American option. It is an option that can be exercised any time in the exercise period such as three months before the expiry date. Pricing will be higher than that of the related European option, but lower than that of an American option with the same expiry date. See *Bermudan option*.

Average rate option

Standard options are exercised when exercise at the strike rate is more beneficial than exercise of the underlying transaction in the cash or spot market. The average rate option pays out if the strike rate is more beneficial than the *average* spot rate over the lifetime of the option. No exercise is involved. Payout is automatic when the average rate is better (higher or lower depending on whether the option is a call or put). The fixings for the average can be monthly, weekly or even daily, and the average does not have to be over the whole option period. Great care must be taken over the fixings. Buyers must assure themselves that the fixings cannot be manipulated. On monthly or quarterly fixings, it would not be too difficult for the underlying exchange rate to be 'disturbed' a few minutes before fixing, only to return to pre-fixing levels afterwards. See also *Non-deliverable forward* for a commentary on this issue. The cost of an average rate option is generally lower than that of a standard option because of the fact that an average is less volatile than the underlying variable.

Basis swap

An interest rate swap (either a cross-currency basis swap or a simple basis swap) in which payments are on a different floating-rate basis, e.g., three-month LIBOR versus six-month LIBOR. Also known as a 'floating/floating swap'. A company can use basis swaps to raise money in the lowest-cost floating-rate market and swap it into its preferred index. Basis swaps can also remove asset/liability mismatch. For example, if a company has liabilities in six-month LIBOR and assets in three-month LIBOR, it can do a three-month/six-month LIBOR swap to match assets and liabilities.

There are other forms of basis swap involving different but

similar types of commodity such as one form of oil versus another – Brent crude versus jet fuel is an example. A basis swap could also involve location differences. The famous 'arbitrage' of Nick Leeson involving the Nikkei index at Osaka Futures exchange being traded against the Nikkei index at the Singapore exchange could have been constructed as a basis swap.

Basket option

A basket option is the right to exchange two or more currencies in a pre-specified combination for a base currency on expiration. As with most options, there can be calls and puts on the basket. One could have regarded an option on the ECU, the forerunner to the euro, as a basket option. A basket option on the ECU would have been cheaper than a series of options on the individual components, DEM, FRF, ESP, etc., as all the individual separate options would perform independently. In the case of the basket, one cannot exercise the DEM component but not the FRF component of the basket. It is all or nothing. The basket may contain synthetic assets or liabilities, positive or negative cash flows in the various currencies and therefore represent an entire balance sheet.

Bermudan option

Similar to an Atlantic option, it is also a cross between a European option and an American option. It is an option that can only be exercised on a series of discrete exercise dates such as the first of every month. As with Atlantic options, pricing will be higher than that of the related European option, but lower than that of an American option with the same expiry date.

Bond option

Option to purchase or sell a particular bond. Exchange-traded options are usually on government bonds. Many bond issues have historically included an embedded bond option. Bonds have for many decades been callable or puttable under certain conditions or could have been redeemed at any time within two dates.

Break forward

One of my inventions in 1984 at Midland Bank! A break forward contract is a forward contract at a forward rate that permits the holder to break or unwind the contract with an opposite transaction at another rate, the break rate. The payoff position is identical to that of a currency option with a deferred premium.

I created it to solve two problems. Companies were reluctant to pay option premiums in advance. Under standard forward contracts, no premiums were payable. Secondly, if the option were not exercised, the premium paid would not be deductible and turn out to be a wasting asset.

Break FRA

Similar to the break forward as applied to interest rate guarantees or IRGs. See *Break forward* and *Interest rate guarantee* and *Forward rate agreement*. Also known as a limit FRA.

Bull floating rate note

See *Reverse floating rate loan*.

Butterfly

Not a financial instrument but a combination of exchange traded options. Simultaneous sale (purchase) of two at-the-money call options and purchase (sale) of one in-the-money call option and one out-of-the-money call option. This is basically a gamble on future volatility.

Fine. But if you want to take a risk, just build the risk profile you want using an appropriate combination of options. Don't bother naming it!

Call option

A call option provides the purchaser with the right, but not the obligation to purchase an underlying asset for cash or in exchange for another asset at a specified price at a specified date or within a specified period.

Callable swap

A swap in which the fixed-rate receiver has the right (but not the obligation) to cancel the swap after or at a certain time. Also known as a 'cancellable swap'. The fixed-rate payer effectively sells the fixed-rate receiver a swaption. The rate paid by the fixed-rate payer is therefore lower. But beware. Sometimes a callable swap provides the fixed-rate payer with the right to terminate the swap. It is better to refer to the fixed-rate payer's right to cancel or the fixed-rate receiver's option. So check the definition for the deal in question before doing the deal. See *Puttable swap*.

Cancellable forward

See *Break forward*.

Cap

In an interest rate cap, in return for the payment of a one-off premium by the buyer, the seller or writer commits to pay to the purchaser the difference between the current interest rate fixing for an interest period and an agreed rate (the strike rate) should market rates rise above that level for the period. Caps are based on a reference index that is fixed at a stated frequency (e.g., three-month LIBOR). Caps can also be regarded as a series of interest rate guarantees (IRGs) or options on FRAs allowing the buyer to take advantage of a reduction in interest rates but providing insurance if rates rise. They are priced as the sum of the cost of the individual IRGs.

Capped swap

See *Limit swap*.

Colander

Working name for break forward. See *Break forward*.

Collar

The simultaneous purchase of a cap and the sale of a floor. The premium for the sale of the floor reduces or eliminates the cost of buying the cap. The premium reduction depends on the strike rate of the two options. If the premium raised by the sale of the floor exactly matches the cost of the cap, the strategy is known misleadingly as a 'zero-cost collar'. But see the entry on the *Zero cost option*. Also known as 'range forward'.

Collared swap

A collar on a swap. The transaction is 'zero-cost' – the purchase of the cap is financed by the sale of the floor. Also a 'range swap'. But beware – as a customer you will be giving away the floor at a bargain rate. It may be cost-free but not value-free.

Commodity cap

A call option on the commodity.

Commodity swap

A swap in which one or both of the payment streams is linked to a commodity. It can be regarded as a cross-currency swap where instead of one of the currencies we have a commodity price index. The swap could be fixed or floating. Usually only the payment streams, not the principal, are exchanged, although physical delivery is becoming increasingly common. Commodity swaps have been traded since the 1970s and enable producers and consumers to hedge commodity prices. Some commodity swaps are used to transfer bonds that are commodity linked. Commodity swaps make sense for commodity producers or consumers to hedge their returns or costs.

Condor

Like the butterfly, this is not a financial product but a combination of options traded on an exchange. The simultaneous purchase of a put and call at the same strike price and the writing of an out of the money put and call. This is another gamble on volatility.

As I wrote above under *Butterfly*, if you want to do something, just do it. Don't worry about what a certain combination of options is called.

Contingent swap

This is a generic expression for a swap that is activated when rates reach a certain level or a specific event occurs. Swaptions may be particular form of contingent swaps. But here the swap has to be exercised under certain conditions. Usually a contingent swap is automatically triggered like a limit swap. Other types of swap, e.g., droplock or spreadlock swaps, are activated only if rates drop to a certain level or if a specified margin over an agreed index is reached.

Cross-currency forward rate agreement

An agreement to buy an FRA in one currency and sell an FRA in another currency. This structure followed the FSA but was a precursor to and supplemented by the exchange rate agreement (ERA) and forward exchange agreement (FXA).

Cross-currency interest rate cap

A cap in which the seller or writer will pay the buyer the spread between two currency indices (usually LIBOR) minus a minimum agreed strike spread, where this exceeds zero. It can therefore be split up into a series of options on forward spread agreements. See *Forward spread agreement (FSA)*.

Cross-currency interest rate swap

The cross-currency interest rate swap involves the exchange of interest rate related cash flows in one currency for those in another over a period of time. Unlike single currency swaps, cross-currency swaps usually do require an exchange of principals on maturity and perhaps at the outset. Both the initial exchange and the final exchange are done at the same spot rate. Cross-currency swaps can be on a fixed/fixed, fixed/floating, or a floating/floating basis.

Currency forward

See *Foreign exchange forward outright*.

Currency swap

There are two forms of currency swap – a cross-currency interest rate swap and a currency swap (traditional). This is not to be confused with the foreign exchange swap (FX swap).

Currency swap (traditional)

A cross-currency swap was traditionally a simple series of foreign exchange forward outright contracts at the same averaged fixed exchange rate exchanging a series of cash flows from one currency into another. Usually such a swap did not involve an exchange of principal amounts at the outset, the spot date. This is now uncommon.

Currency option

See *Option* and *Option dated forward contract*.

Cylinder

The simultaneous purchase of a currency put option and sale of a currency call option at different strike prices. Both options are out-of-the-money. This strategy enables purchasers to hedge their downside risk at a reduced cost. This is at the expense of forgoing upside beyond a certain level since the selling of the call finances the purchase of the put (or *vice versa*). Also see *Range forward*.

Deferred swap

A swap in which the payments are deferred for a specified period. Unlike a forward swap, where the entire swap is delayed, in a deferred swap only the payments are deferred. For example, a company wanting to enter a swap, but not wanting cash flows until a future period, may want to defer payment.

Delayed LIBOR reset swap

Also known as a 'LIBOR-in-arrears swap'. A swap in which the current floating payment is based on the LIBOR rate for the next period. These swaps can be used if a floating-rate payer considers that rates are coming down in the short-term.

Differential swap

A swap in which a counterparty swaps floating payments referenced to an interest rate of one currency into floating payments referenced to an interest rate of another currency. The principal for both payments, however, is in one currency. The differential swap is therefore a strip of forward rate agreements and the pricing characteristics are similar to a fixed/fixed cross-currency swap, and a premium will be payable either upfront or as a spread on the floating rate.

Digital swap

A swap structure where the swap can be extended or cancelled after a given number of years. Equivalent to a swap plus a European swaption expiring at the date when the extension choice is made.

Discount swap

An off-market swap in which the fixed payments are below the market rate. At the end of the swap the shortfall is made up by one large payment. Companies may use this type of structure to reduce interest rate payments during completion of a project. The more these payments are discounted, the more credit risk is taken by the counterparty. At the extreme, fixed payments can be set to zero, resulting in a larger balloon payment on the maturity date. This is known as a zero coupon swap.

Dual-currency bond

A bond where the coupons are paid in one currency, but the principal is redeemed in another.

Dual-currency swap

A swap used to hedge dual-currency bonds in which the issuer has the option to repay principal and coupon in either the base currency or an alternative currency, at a pre-set exchange rate. Dual-currency swaps are currency swaps that incorporate the foreign exchange options necessary to hedge the interest payments back into the principal currency.

Embedded option

An option embedded in another host security, usually a debt. Examples include structured notes, mortgage-backed securities and callable bonds.

Escalating principal swap

See *Accreting swap.*

Escalating rate swap

A swap in which the fixed-rate payments increase over time. This may be used by companies with tight liquidity that expect cash flow to improve in the future.

European option

An option that can only be exercised on the expiration date.

Exchange rate agreement (ERA)

A synthetic agreement for a forward exchange swap originally launched by Barclays Bank in 1987. It is settled by reference to the forward premium or discount at maturity but ignores the spot rate outcome. See *Forward spread agreement (FSA), Spread agreement on forward exchange (SAFE), Forward exchange agreement (FXA).*

Exit option

An exit option is an option to get out of a structure. For example, an exit option on a swap allows you enter into an offsetting position at a certain date, so it represents a swaption on the offsetting swap.

Extendible swap

A swap in which the fixed-rate payer has an option to extend the swap for a further period. A three-year swap extendible for a further two years would simply use a three-year swap in conjunction with a three-year option into a two-year swap. This may be used by a company that is unsure of future financing requirements but wants access to future funding at the same cost.

Fixed/floating swap

See *Interest rate swap*.

Flexible forward

See *Range forward* or *Break forward*. As in all such brand-named products it is imperative that the buyer has no doubt what he is buying.

Floating/floating swap

See *Basis swap*.

Floating rate note (FRN)

A floating rate note is a bond with the coupon payments floating in relation to a market yardstick such as six-month LIBOR. But I have seen a fixed rate note called an FRN!

Floor

A contract whereby the seller agrees to pay the purchaser the difference between current interest rates and an agreed rate (the strike rate) should interest rates fall below the agreed level. Floors are based on a reference index such as six-month LIBOR, and are effectively a strip of interest-rate options. The value of the floor is the combined value of this strip of options on FRAs also known as interest-rate guarantees or IRGs. Floors provide a hedge for those investors wanting to preserve a certain return on their floating rate assets.

Foreign exchange forward outright

A foreign exchange forward outright is often just known as a forward contract, forward exchange contract (FEC) or a forward outright. An agreement to exchange a specified amount of one currency for another at a future date at an agreed rate. The foreign exchange forward outright rate for the exchange of currencies is priced on an arbitrage-free basis according to the market interest rates in the two currencies. If the foreign exchange swap is the original financial derivative, then the forward outright is the original structured financial product. In most instances, the foreign exchange forward is not an interbank product but a customer product. It is made up of a foreign exchange spot contract plus a foreign exchange swap. The FEC involves one exchange of principals at a forward date whilst the FX swap involves two exchanges, one now and the other at the forward date.

Foreign exchange spot

A foreign exchange spot contract is not really a derivative. It is an agreement to exchange one currency with another at a certain rate for value at the spot date. The spot date is almost always two business days forward from the date of dealing. But sometimes, as in the case of Korea, spot can be one business day forward.

Foreign exchange swap (FX swap)

A foreign exchange swap is the original financial derivative and was for many years just known as a swap. It is an agreement to exchange two currencies for value spot and to exchange them back at another rate at a forward date. The difference in the exchange rates between the spot and forward legs of the FX swap will be the forward spread agreed under the FX swap. There should be minimal difference between holding a currency at its fixed interest rate for a certain period and, on the other hand, swapping the currency under the FX swap and investing in the other currency at its fixed rate for the period. The FX swap would involve a package deal – the sale now and the pre-agreed buyback of the currency later.

Forward band

See *Range forward*.

Forward exchange agreement (FXA)

A synthetic agreement for a forward exchange swap. It is settled by reference to the spot rate as well as the forward premium or discount. Launched by Midland Bank in 1987. The ERA launched weeks earlier, ignored the spot rate. See *Forward spread agreement (FSA)*, *Spread agreement on forward exchange (SAFE)*, *Exchange rate agreement (ERA)*.

Forward exchange contract (FEC) *or* Forward contract

See *Foreign exchange forward outright*.

Forward exchange rate agreement (FERA)

Not to be confused with forward exchange agreement (FXA) or forward rate agreement or forward spread agreement. It is a forward exchange contract that does not lead to exchange of principal amounts at the maturity of the contract but is cash settled. The forward exchange rate agreement was developed in the mid-1980s and is the precursor to the non-deliverable forward contract. The rationale behind the FERA was to assist with balance sheet translation exposure. See *Non-deliverable forward*.

Forward interest rate swap

A swap in which the fixed coupon is set before the start date. If a company expects rates to rise soon but only needs funds later, it may enter into a forward interest rate swap. Also known as a forward start swap.

Forward rate agreement (FRA)

A forward rate agreement, or FRA, is an agreement between two parties who want to protect themselves against future movements in interest rates. By entering into an FRA, the parties lock in an interest rate for a stated period of time starting on a future settlement date, based on a specified notional principal amount. The buyer of the FRA enters into the contract to protect itself from a future increase in interest rates. This occurs when a company believes that interest rates may rise and wants to fix its borrowing cost today. The seller of the FRA wants to protect itself from a future decline in interest rates. Investors who want to hedge the return obtained on a future deposit use this strategy.

Forward spread agreement (FSA)

The counterparties of a forward spread agreement contract into a spread between two forward rate agreement rates applied to a nominal amount of one currency on the same basis. The settlement amount will be the difference between the settlement reference spread rate minus the contracted spread rate calculated on a 360-day basis.

FOX

Just two weeks after Midland Bank launched the break forward, Hambros Bank announced the FOX – a forward contract with an optional exit. See *Break forward*.

Future rate agreement

Usually called a 'forward rate agreement'. By and large, the word 'future' applies to contracts on derivative exchanges such as LIFFE or the IMM, and 'forward' applies to OTC products.

FX collar

See *Range forward*.

FX swap

See *Foreign exchange swap*.

Icelandic option

See *Atlantic option*.

Interest rate cap

See *Cap*.

Interest rate guarantee (IRG)

An option on a forward rate agreement. Purchasers have the right, but not the obligation, to fix an interest rate for a specified future period. A cap can be thought of as a strip of interest rate guarantees. See *Cap*.

Interest rate swap

An interest rate swap is a contractual agreement between two counterparties to exchange cash flows on particular dates in the future. The most common type of swap or 'plain vanilla' swap involves one party, the fixed rate payer, making fixed payments, and the other party, the floating rate payer, making payments which depend on the level of future interest rates. The swap agreement stipulates all of the conditions and definitions required to administer the swap including the notional principal amount, fixed coupon, accrual methods, day count methods, effective date, terminating date, cash flow frequency, compounding frequency, and basis for the floating index. Interest rate payments are made on a notional amount and there is no exchange of principal. Interest rate swaps provide users with a means of hedging the effects of changing interest rates by changing the basis on which they pay or receive interest flows. For example, a company can convert floating-rate interest payments to fixed-rate payments if it thinks interest rates are set to rise. It can also use swaps to cut down mismatches between its assets and liabilities.

Kick-in forward

With a kick-in forward, an 'in-strike' is selected. If and when the spot rate reaches the in-strike rate at any time during the option period, the option automatically turns into a forward contract. It is cheaper than a standard European or American option as it never becomes in-the-money. It is effectively an option on a forward with automatic exercise when it becomes at-the-money.

Kick-in option

A kick-in option is similar to a knock-in option. An 'in-strike' is selected in addition to the normal strike rate. Only if and when the spot rate reaches the in-strike rate, at any time during the option period, does the option come into effect. See *Knock-in option*.

Knock-in option

With a knock-in option, an 'in-strike' is selected in addition to the normal strike rate. Only if and when the spot rate reaches the in-strike rate, at any time during the option period, does the option come into effect. The in-strike rate is set at a level so that the option is out of the money at the outset. Because of the necessity to satisfy the condition of reaching the in-strike rate, the in-strike option is cheaper than standard options. See *Kick-in option*.

Knock-out forward

A relatively new name but very much the same as the break forward invented in the mid-1980s. But here the knock-out forward provides a more beneficial forward rate for the customer rather than an adverse rate for the customer under the fixed rate in the break forward. But then the selling bank benefits if and when the 'out-strike', similar to the break rate in the break forward, is reached by the market rate. In the break forward, the customer has the right to break the forward contract should the break rate reach the market rate.

Knock-out option

As with the knock-in option, with a knock-out option, an 'out-strike' is selected in addition to the normal strike rate. Here, if and when the spot rate reaches the out-strike rate at any time during the option period, the option becomes void. The out-strike rate is set at a level so that the option is out of the money when the spot rate reaches the out-strike rate. Because of the possibility of the option being cancelled before it is used, the out-strike option is cheaper than a standard option.

Limit FRA

Similar to the break forward as applied to interest rate guarantees or IRGs. Also known as a 'break FRA'. See *Break FRA*.

Limit swap

This is the interest rate swap version of the break forward. It is a swap with a cap in which the floating payments of a swap are capped at a certain level. A floating-rate counterparty can thereby limit its exposure to rising interest rates above a certain level. Also known as a capped swap.

Mortgage swap

This is a form of asset swap and similar in structure to an amortizing swap. The swap is linked to mortgage payments where the notional principal amortizes in line with the mortgage principal. These swaps may use a standard annuity formula to fix outstanding principal, or they may use some estimate of mortgage prepayment given the level of interest rates.

Non-deliverable currency option

A non-deliverable currency option has the same properties as a standard currency option except that on exercise there is cash settlement and no exchange of currencies. These are used where exchange controls or lack of currency liquidity make obtaining one or both currencies difficult.

Non-deliverable currency swap

A non-deliverable currency swap has the same properties as a standard currency swap except that on the payment dates only a difference payment is made. One or both of the currencies are valued using an exchange rate fixing and translated and settled in a convertible currency.

Non-deliverable forward (NDF)

A forward exchange contract that does not lead to the exchange of principal amounts at the maturity of the contract. Similar in concept to FRAs, they are contracts for differences. FRAs fix interest rates, whilst NDFs fix exchange rates. The contract exchange rate is compared with the exchange rate fixing on the fixing date (two business days before settlement) and a settlement is made based on that amount. They were first seen in the mid-1980s as forward exchange rate agreements. Main uses are to avoid exchange controls, translation exposure hedging and settlement risk minimization.

But buyer beware. Do not agree to an exchange rate fixing mechanism that can be manipulated by the counterparty. It is very difficult, but not impossible, to manipulate the LIBOR fixing for interest rates. Moving the market quite substantially a few seconds before an exchange rate fixing is quite easy.

Option

An option gives the holder the right but not the obligation to buy or sell a commodity or a currency for a specified cash value in a specified currency on a specified date or range of dates. A warrant is a standardized option listed on a exchange.

Option combination strategy

Option positions may be combined to create a net pay-off profile that corresponds to the risk/reward profile of the investor or position-taker. Based on an investor's viewpoint, he can implement various strategies that utilize combinations of options and futures to manage pay-offs and option premiums. Some examples of option strategies include spreads, combinations, straddles, strangles, condors, etc. These are not products as such but packages of products traded on derivatives exchanges.

Option-dated forward contract

An option-dated forward contract is a forward exchange contract where the customer has the right to choose when to exchange currencies between two specified dates. This allows for delays in shipment or payment of underlying trade transactions.

Option fence

An asset plus a range forward or collar.

Participating cap

The simultaneous purchase of an out-of-the-money cap and the sale of a lesser amount of an in-the-money floor. Because the in-the-money floor is worth more, the purchaser of a participating cap sells less floors for a 'zero-cost' combination and can therefore derive some benefit if rates fall. Although the purchaser would not derive as much benefit if rates fell as would have been the case with a straightforward cap, he does not have to pay a premium.

Participating forward

The simultaneous purchase of a call (put) and sale of a put (call) at the same strike price. The option purchased must be out of the money and the option sold (to finance the option purchase) is for a smaller amount but in the money. See *Break forward*.

Participating swap

A swap in which floating-rate exposure is hedged, but in which the hedger still retains some benefit from a fall in rates.

Payer's swaption

A payer's swaption provides the purchaser the right, but not the obligation to pay a specified fixed rate for a series of pay dates and notional principal amounts outstanding at those dates.

Perpetual FRN

An FRN with no maturity date. They were very fashionable in late 1987 as a means of raising bank capital. But then the market collapsed as investors realized that, as there was no maturity date, liquidation of their investments depended on someone else buying them. The music stopped and fingers were burned. One day no doubt somebody will successfully sell a zero-coupon perpetual bond!

Put option

A put option provides the purchaser with the right, but not the obligation to sell an underlying asset for cash or in exchange for another asset at a specified price at a specified date or within a specified period.

Put spread

A put spread reduces the cost of buying a put by selling another put at a lower level. This limits the amount the purchaser can gain if the underlying goes down, but the premium received from selling an out of-the-money put partly finances the at-the-money put.

Puttable swap

A swap in which the fixed-rate payer has the right (but not the obligation) to cancel the swap after or at a certain time. The fixed-rate payer effectively buys from the fixed-rate receiver a swaption. The rate paid by the fixed-rate payer is therefore higher. But beware. Sometimes a puttable swap does the opposite. It provides the fixed-rate receiver with the right to terminate the swap. So check the definition for the deal in question before doing the deal. It is better to refer to the fixed-rate payer's right to cancel or the fixed-rate receiver's option. See *Callable swap*. Also known as a 'cancellable swap'.

Range forward

A FX collar using forward contracts that replicates the payoff profile of purchasing an in-the-money call and selling an in-the-money put.

For example if the forward price for sterling is USD1.50, a range forward can be produced by buying a forward contract to purchase sterling at USD1.50, entering a forward contract where the buyer has the right to break the contract at a price of USD1.43, and the seller of the forward contract has the right to break the contract at a price of USD1.56.

Rate cap

A contract where the holder has several consecutive calls options on a series of forward rates for a period of time. If rates rise, the holder receives a benefit upon automatic exercise of each in-the-money call and can apply that benefit to the cost of servicing an outstanding loan – hence the term 'cap'.

Rate floor

A contract where the holder has several consecutive put options on a series of forward rates for a period of time. If rates fall, the holder receives a benefit upon automatic exercise of each in-the-money put and can apply that benefit to the diminished return earned on floating rate assets – hence the term 'floor'.

Receiver's swaption

A receiver's swaption provides the purchaser the right, but not the obligation to receive a specified fixed rate for a series of pay dates and notional principal amounts outstanding at those dates.

Reverse floating rate loan

Combination of a conventional fixed rate loan and a swap to pay fixed and receive floating. Therefore, if floating rates rise, the net coupon payment falls.

Reverse floating swap

A swap in which the floating payments are inversely proportional to interest rates.

Reversible swap

A swap in which one side has an option to alter the payment basis (fixed/floating) after a certain period. This is usually achieved by the use of a swaption, allowing the purchaser the opportunity to enter a swap with payment on the opposite basis. The swaption would be for twice the principal amount, one half of which nullifies the original swap.

Roller coaster swap

A swap where the notional principal amount goes up and down. Sometimes defined as a swap in which one counterparty alternates between paying fixed and paying floating.

Seasonal swap

A swap in which the principal alternates between zero and some notional principal amount. The principal amount of the swap is designed to hedge the seasonal borrowing needs of a company. Retail companies might use such swaps to fix rates on loans required only on a seasonal basis, e.g., for building up inventory.

Spread agreement on forward exchange (SAFE)

A synthetic agreement for a forward exchange swap. The settlement amount is either by reference to the forward premium or discount on maturity only (ERA style), or both the forward premium and the spot rate outcome (FXA style). This composite product was governed by the British Bankers Association in 1987 after the launches of the rival FXA and ERA. So as to provide standard market terms and, therefore, liquidity to the concept. See *Forward spread agreement (FSA)*, *Forward exchange agreement (FXA)*, *Exchange rate agreement (ERA)*.

Spreadlock swap

A swap in which one payment stream is referenced at a fixed spread over a benchmark rate such as US treasuries.

Staged drawdown swap

See *Accreting swap*.

STIRS

Short-term interest rate futures.

Straddle

An option strategy whereby the purchaser of a straddle buys a put option and a call option with the same strike price on the underlying. Although the purchaser pays two premiums, he benefits if the underlying moves a certain amount in either direction. In essence, this investor is anticipating an increase in price volatility during the term of the option strategy.

Strangle

An option strategy whereby the purchaser of a strangle buys a put option and a call option on the same instrument, but at strike prices equally out-of-the-money. The strangle costs less than the straddle because both options are out-of-the-money, but profits are only generated if the underlying moves dramatically.

Or is it the other way around? I never could remember the difference between a straddle and a strangle! What is it that you are trying to achieve? Put the appropriate combination of derivatives together and call it what you like.

Swap

See *Foreign exchange swap, Currency swap, Interest rate swap.*

Swaption

An interest rate swaption is an option on a forward start swap to either pay or receive a fixed rate. Because there are two parties to a swap, the floating payer and the fixed payer, the swaption buyer has to make clear which leg of the swap he wants to enter. The right to pay fixed is called a 'payer's swaption'. The right to receive fixed is called a 'receiver's swaption'. Original interest arose from the issuance of bonds with embedded put features. Often, the price of the bond did not fully reflect the fair value of the embedded option, and the issuer would sell a swaption to obtain a lower fixed cost of funds. Alternatively, a significant percentage of these debt issues are swapped out to obtain sub-LIBOR funding. In these cases the issuer needs a facility to cancel the swap if the bonds are not put or called. To eliminate this exposure, the companies would enter into a swaption to offset the underlying swap.

Tunnel

See *Cylinder.*

Warrant

A certificate, often issued together with a bond, giving the purchaser the right but not the obligation, to purchase a specified amount of an asset at a certain price over a specified period of time. Such assets include equity, debt, currencies and commodities.

Warrant-driven swap

A swap with a warrant allowing an issuer of a bond the extension of a swap in the event that it exercises a similar warrant on the bond. See *Extendible swap.*

Yield curve swap

A swap in which the two interest streams reflect different points on the yield curve. For example, one side could pay the five-year constant maturity treasury rate versus the two-year constant maturity rate. The swap can be on either a fixed or a floating basis. Many investors who have a point of view on the shape of the yield curve have used this, as have debt managers that want to hedge a structured note issue.

Zero-cost option

Any combination of options that involves financing an option bought by the simultaneous sale of another of equal cost. See *Collar*, *Cylinder* and *Participating forward*. The package deal should (in theory) be a good deal cheaper for the bank and, therefore the customer, than doing both transactions separately.

But always remember – there is an enormous difference between something being cheaper and costing less money! The 'zero cost' option combination involves the 'simultaneous sale of another of equal cost'. The problem for the customer is that this sale of an option to the bank will not be of equivalent value. It will be adjusted to provide the bank's profit.

Zero-coupon bond

A bond with no interest paid through the life of the bond. The initial price is therefore at a deep discount to the face value payable on maturity.

Zero-coupon perpetual bond

I dreamt about selling one of these but never did. But I did announce the zero-coupon perpetual bond as a new product on an April Fool's Day. I received quite a few enquiries. But some equally strange products have been sold. *Caveat emptor*. See *Perpetual FRN*.

Zero-coupon swap

A swap in which either or both of the counterparties makes one payment at maturity. More usually it is only the fixed-rate payments that are deferred. The party not receiving payment until maturity obviously incurs a greater credit risk than it would with a plain vanilla swap. The swap is advantageous for a company that will not receive payment for a project until it is completed, or to hedge zero-coupon liabilities, such as zero-coupon bonds.

Appendix 3: Risk management terms

Accreting

Denotes an increase in the underlying principal over the life of an instrument. As in accreting cap, accreting collar, accreting swap, accreting swaption, etc.

Arrears set rate

A rate fixed two business days before the end of an interest period and paid at the end of that interest period. Also known as 'backset rate'.

Amortizing

Denotes a reduction in the underlying principal over the life of an instrument. As in amortizing cap, amortizing collar, amortizing swap, amortizing swaption, etc.

Backset rate

See *Arrears set rate*.

Basis

The difference between the spot cash market price and the price of a futures or forward contract on the same underlying financial instrument.

Basis point

One hundredth of one per cent.

BBA

British Bankers Association sets the BBAISR used for most derivative fixings. In 1984 the BBA produced legal terms and conditions for three early derivatives, FRABBA terms for FRAs, LICOM for currency options and swap terms. It later produced SAFEBBA terms for SAFEs. The BBA terms are now seldom used and have been supplanted by ISDA terms.

BBAISR

The British Bankers Association interest settlement rate is the LIBOR set by a panel of 16 London banks and used by most derivative contracts. Beware of a contract that uses a LIBOR that is not BBAISR. The BBAISR is the most widespread benchmark for derivatives, and therefore provides liquidity and the ability to hedge internationally. There must be a very good reason (to *your* and not just your banker's benefit) to use another LIBOR. BBAISR eliminates the top two and bottom two banks and is rounded to five decimal places.

Break-even forward rate

See *Implied forward rate*. It is the theoretical breakeven re-investment rate used to re-invest the proceeds of a short-term investment to obtain an equivalent maturity value as with one long-term investment of a period equal to that on the short-term investment plus the re-investment period.

Cock dates

Cock dates refer to non-standardized maturity dates of contracts such as maturity on dates such as three and a half months from deal dates.

ERM

The ERM is the exchange rate mechanism giving rise to the euro, replacing the national currencies of most of the EU countries.

EURIBOR

EURIBOR, the European interbank offer rate, is the 'domestic' index rate used for fixing the euro. It is the rate at which prime banks lend to other prime banks in the Eurozone financial centres from one- to 12-month deposits in domestic euros. This has replaced FIBOR, MIBOR, MIBOR and PIBOR (Frankfurt, Madrid, Milan and Paris)

The EURIBOR is calculated by the Brussels-based European Banking Federation, but fixed at 11:30 Brussels time, disseminated at 11:00, using rates obtained from a panel of 57 prime banks. 15 per cent of the quotations at the top and bottom are eliminated. It is set on day D for a value date of D+2, using an actual/360 day-count convention. Despite the fact that EURIBOR is a domestic rate, there are several banks in the panel based in London.

EURO-LIBOR will be an 'offshore' rate or euro-euro rate quoted in London. See *LIBOR* and *Eurocurrency*. LIFFE is suitably hedging its bets by offering contracts in EURIBOR and in EURO-LIBOR, but in January 1999, the trading in EURO-LIBOR contracts at LIFFE was only 20 per cent of EURIBOR contracts. Note that EURIBOR is fixed at 10:00 London time compared with 11:00 for EURO-LIBOR.

Eurocurrency

A eurocurrency is currency traded outside the country of the currency. Eurodollars are US dollars in London or Tokyo and Euromarks are D-marks in New York or London. Euro euros will be euros traded in New York, Tokyo and whilst sterling is outside the eurozone, in London.

HIBOR

HIBOR is the Hong Kong interbank offer rate. See *LIBOR*.

Implied forward rate

See *Break-even forward rate*. The implied forward rate is the forward rate obtained and implied by borrowing for long-term and lending short-term (or *vice versa*). It is the basis for the determination of interest rate futures and FRA contracts. It is crucially different from the break-even forward rate in that the implied forward rate is not theoretical. It is based on actual transactions including margins above and below LIBOR on the borrowing and deposit. The break-even forward rate uses the bid rate (or the offer rate) for both the short-term and the long-term transactions.

Interest period

The period used for calculation of the settlement amount on a derivative, using the notional principal amount due, the contract rate and the fixing rate.

IPMA

The International Primary Market Association is a London-based trade body which represents underwriters of debt and equity securities.

ISDA

International Swap and Derivatives Association. When ISDA was founded in the mid-1980s, it was called the International Swap Dealers Association. Its primary purpose at the time was to formulate standard legal documentation for swaps.

LIBOR

LIBOR is the London interbank offer rate. LIBOR rate is a tautology. LIBOR is the rate at which prime banks in London offer to lend to other prime banks in London, traditionally at 11:00 London time. LIFFE uses the BBAISR.

Other than for sterling, LIBOR is set on day D for a value date of D+2. There is no short answer to the question 'What is today's LIBOR?' There is a LIBOR for most major currencies and all standard terms from one-month to one-year. It is extremely important to negotiate the LIBOR definition in contracts. Factors that affect LIBOR are the creditworthiness of the panel, the number of banks in the panel, the fixing time and the rounding mechanism.

Of late, a LIBOR reference including a Japanese bank has tended to be higher than the index without one. So much so, that The Singapore International Monetary Exchange, SIMEX, has launched a three-month euroyen LIBOR futures contract in addition to the contract it has traded settled using the Tokyo rate, TIBOR. SIMEX said that the launch of the additional contract was in response to requests from members and their customers as a result of the divergence between LIBOR and TIBOR.

LIBOR fixed at a time when there is limited liquidity in London would also be higher. In the rounding mechanism LIBOR can be rounded up, down or to the nearest one-eighth, one-sixteenth or to five decimal places. So exercise great caution with respect to the definition of LIBOR. I once conceded 2 basis points to a borrowing bank, but in the documentation inserted LIBOR rounding up to higher one-eighth per cent and with a Japanese bank! See *BBAISR* and *EURIBOR*.

LIFFE

The London International Financial Futures Exchange.

Optimal date of exercise

For American-style options it may be advantageous to exercise before the option expiry date. If so, then the most advantageous early exercise date is the optimal date of exercise.

OTC

Over-the-counter as opposed to exchange-traded. This applies to contracts entered into between two counterparties acting as principals, one of which is probably a bank for market, tax or regulatory reasons. Such OTC contracts are, in general, not standardized in terms of maturity or expiry dates or principal amounts. Nevertheless, customers will usually obtain finer prices for round amounts and standard dates. See *Cock dates*.

SIBOR

SIBOR is the Singapore interbank offer rate. See *LIBOR*.

Spot

Two business days forward in the financial centres of the two currencies concerned in a foreign exchange contract or the financial centre of the only currency in the case of an interest rate contract.

TIBOR

TIBOR is the Tokyo interbank offer rate. See *LIBOR*.

Transaction currency exposure

Transaction exposure is the exposure arising through the purchase or sale of goods or services in a foreign currency. And this may not necessarily be cross-border. British firms will incur transaction exposure within the UK if they sell products to larger firms in the UK in the euro even if sterling does not join the European single currency.

Translation currency exposure

Translation exposure is the potential for change in the value in the home currency of foreign-currency-denominated assets or liabilities. Even an individual can incur considerable translation exposure. Borrowing in a low-interest rate foreign currency may seem sensible. But should the foreign currency appreciate significantly, then the borrower might have difficulty in repaying.

I was once told by the Finance Director of a prominent Asian university that he was going to borrow in low-interest US dollars to save interest costs. I advised him strongly against it as low-cost was not the same as inexpensive. A month after I gave him that advice, his currency depreciated by more than 50 per cent.

Vanilla

Venezuelan Vanilla from the town of Guiria has the most extraordinary flavour. However, in the financial markets, it means 'standard' or 'ordinary' as opposed to exotic or 'third-generation'. Don't be embarrassed into using something new to be 'with-it'. Vanilla is usually good enough and, other than for reasons such as tax, regulation or a sucker investor, is usually best value.

Happy the man who far from schemes of business, like the early generations of mankind, ploughs and ploughs again his ancestral land with oxen of his own breeding, with no yoke of usury on his neck.

HORACE

Those who devour usury will not stand except as stands one whom the Evil One by his touch hath driven to madness. That is because they say: 'Trade is like usury but Allah hath permitted trade and forbidden usury.' Those who after receiving direction from their Lord desist shall be pardoned for the past; their case is for Allah (to judge); but those who repeat (the offence) are companions of the fire: they will abide therein (for ever).

THE KORAN: SURAH 2, VERSE 275

Appendix 4: Islamic financial products

Background

The London *Sunday Times* of 2 February 1997 wrote: 'The advent of Islamic Finance will be a Godsend for them [*Islamic clients*]. It could also turn out to be a goldmine for the United Bank of Kuwait.'

There seems to be considerable demand for such Islamic banking products both in Islamic countries and in the West. To date, for a number of reasons including risk aversion and conservatism, this need has gone largely unfilled.

The purpose of this appendix is to provide an introduction to 'Islamic' banking. It does not attempt to provide a moral justification, rationale or even establish clear rules as to what is Islamic and therefore *Hallal* and what is un-Islamic and therefore prohibited or *Haram*. But even if the reader has little interest in Islamic Banking *per se* there are important lessons to be learned from the creative process used to satisfy the Islamic regulations. There are numerous parallels with tax-driven structuring in conventional banking markets. Throughout this appendix there are references to familiar Western financial instruments.

Overview

It is simply an accepted fact that there are sufficient Muslim investors and borrowers in both Islamic and non-Islamic countries to warrant the attention of traditional banks who seek to serve such clients and capture a potentially profitable slice of a still relatively untapped market. Just as interesting and useful for non-Islamic bankers are the lessons learned from the innovation and creativity applied in meeting Islamic criteria.

This appendix serves to clear away some of the mystery and show how some such financial products can fit alongside a conventional interest-bearing banking system and thereby serve a Western bank's retail and wholesale clients or help a corporation that is offered Islamic funds. Some non-Islamic financial or exporting institutions may also find it prudent to use Islamic finance so as to curry favour in Islamic markets, thereby easing entry or enhancing business.

Some products are more Islamic than others. The basic principle is that interest usury or *Riba* used interchangeably is prohibited on the principle of no pain, no gain. What I, as a non-Islamic observer would call 'pure' Islamic banking, appears to be structurally very similar to venture capital finance, non-recourse project finance or ordinary equity investment. The investor takes a share in the profits, if any, of the venture and is liable to lose his capital. It involves investing, but not lending, and therefore on a systemic basis is similar to the German, Japanese and Spanish banking systems rather than the British or American systems.

Just as in tax management, however, numerous products have been developed to meet the letter but not necessarily the spirit of the regulations. There are a number of grey areas. Some products that might have been acceptable 20 years ago are no longer so. Just as in the process of converting interest into capital gains for tax purposes, early Islamic investors were content to enter into zero-coupon bonds or discounted Treasury bills and receive the interest forgone in the form of capital gains.

In the mid-1980s I dealt in foreign exchange and deposit packaged transactions. The 'Islamic' client bought a low-interest-rate currency or even gold from the bank. This was placed on deposit free of interest with the bank. At the same time, the currency or gold was sold forward. But the forward rate was adjusted to reflect the fact that no interest is paid on the deposit account. The purchase, deposit and forward transaction had to be done as a package to meet the Bank of England's rules on forward transactions at off-market rates. I have also transacted three-party circular transactions that generate locked-in returns for the 'Islamic' party.

Such locked-in and predetermined capital gains are in most fiscal jurisdictions now regarded as interest for tax purposes rather than capital gains which is either free of tax or favourably taxed. Deep discount or deep gain legislation is continually being fine-tuned in many countries including the UK. Similarly such devices of converting *Riba* to capital gains are, in the most blatant forms, increasingly unacceptable to the Islamic authorities. Nevertheless, in my observations of the market, 95 per cent of Islamic banking as practised involves some form of pre-determination of profit or 'mark-up' that, whilst acceptable to individual Islamic authorities, would now be regarded as capital gains to most fiscal authorities. But it is not for me to suggest that all such pre-determination is *Haram*. For some institutions, appearances are important in terms of being seen to be Islamic in the eyes of their customers, share-holders and regulators. And even when there is a guaranteed return generated through a 'mark-up' scheme, the linking to an underlying trade transaction is deemed 'a good thing'. In a Western banking system, commercial paper and bankers' acceptances need in theory to have an underlying trade transaction. In practice the link to trade is often weak.

Just as there is no central, global fiscal authority, there is no Islam-wide authority that determines what is *Hallal* and what is *Haram*. There is a danger that some banks will go around 'opinion-hunting' to get Islamic approval for their schemes. I am far from suggesting that the system is corrupt. The same sort of process happens in the form of 'opinion-shopping' by banks with the big-five accounting bodies or with various tax counsel on interest-bearing structured finance schemes. Such a process is natural or just inevitable. Furthermore, just as Western banking business moves from one tax jurisdiction to another, so does Islamic banking in its less than pure forms seek approval for various schemes from more lenient authorities.

Beyond the question of interest/*Riba* is the ethical issue.

Islamic investments exclude tobacco, alcohol, gaming and other 'undesirable' sectors. Islamic investors, by and large, are motivated in their choice of investments by much the same criteria as their Western ethical counterparts. The search for acceptable investments is balanced by natural risk-aversion. Islamic borrowers, on the other hand, also demonstrate a reluctance to give away a share in the profits of their enterprise. It is not therefore surprising that most Islamic banking takes the form of one type of mark-up or other rather than profit sharing.

But Islamic banking is still very much a fledgling industry with only 20 years of practice. Compare the total value of Islamic Banks globally of USD166 billion to say Citigroup in excess of USD1 trillion. The mark-up method is favoured for a number of reasons; it is simple in design, profitable in return and its short-term nature is ideal for managing liquidity in a market with little or no interbank facility. Islamic banks generally do not generally have the infrastructure or capabilities to compete with *Haram* products. Faith alone does not appear to be sufficient. ABC Islamic Bank have addressed the liquidity problem with a daily valued equity unit trust. ABC offer two funds. The ABC clearing company operates on a daily basis, with the ABC Islamic Fund on a weekly basis. In the case of the former, gains are granted to the depositor but in the event of a loss, the facility is underwritten by ABC as guarantor, providing the investor with his principal sum. In the case of the latter, the participation is sold on termination and all gains and losses are borne by the depositor.

The mechanics are such that if you have excess monies, you purchase a portion. When the money is required you sell. If there is an increase in the value of share you benefit, if not, you lose. In any case, some deem this un-Islamic, for there is no true participation in the element of risk regarding the companies involved. To me, this sort of structure is similar to the approved *Musharaka* product but diversified through the bank rather than creating a self-diversified portfolio.

A brief history

Small-scale 'interest-free' savings banks were created from 1963 in Egypt. They were not overtly Islamic for fear of offending the political authorities. These savings banks neither paid interest to their depositors nor charged interest to their borrowers, investing mainly in trade and industry. The banks' depositors were paid a share of the profits of the borrowers, acting like savings and loan institutions rather than commercial banks. The Nasr Social Bank, established in Egypt in 1971, was created as an interest-free commercial bank, but still without specific reference to Islam.

The Islamic Development Bank (IDB) was established by the conference of Islamic finance ministers in Jeddah in December 1973. The inaugural meeting of the board was in July 1975 and the Bank opened for business on 20 October 1975. The IDB was created as an intergovernmental bank aimed at providing development funds for projects in less well off member countries. The IDB provides fee-based financial services and profit-sharing financial assistance. The IDB operations, which are generally free of interest, are explicitly based on *Shariah* principles. The bank does, nonetheless, engage in depositing its funds in interest-bearing placements, as a facility for surplus funds. The bank does not make grants but provides temporary assistance, i.e., the capital is revolving, replenishing itself. Hence the preference to short-term trade finance as opposed to long-term development, where benefits only present themselves after many years.

Gradually overtly Islamic banks were developed in the Middle East through the late 1970s, such as the Dubai Islamic Bank, the Faisal Islamic Bank of Sudan, the Faisal Islamic Bank of Egypt, and the Bahrain Islamic Bank. Islamic banks were also developed in Malaysia, and even in predominantly Catholic Philippines to serve the Muslim population in Mindanao and in India. Luxembourg has the Islamic Finance House, DMI is based in Geneva, and there are Islamic financial institutions in Denmark, Australia and in South Africa. There are also developments being encouraged by the Central Banks of Nigeria and Indonesia.

To my knowledge, whilst Western banks such as ANZ and HSBC have Islamic Banking units, the focus of attention has largely been in serving clients in Islamic countries. Muslim clients in the West are not served except by relatively small and lowly rated specialist Islamic banks. With regards to ANZ, one of their vehicles is FAIM, First ANZ International Murabaha Ltd. Also it is interesting to note that these 'Islamic' activities are integrated in the normal accounts of the bank. There is no specific segregated Islamic Division as, for example, the Islamic Banking Unit of the United Bank of Kuwait.

Basic principles

The basic aspect of Islamic banking is the absence of interest, but there are other social and ethical features claimed by the more 'pure' or 'zealous', such as aiding a more equitable distribution of income and wealth and avoiding undesirable areas. Some argue that the prohibition of *Riba* is akin to the usury laws in many Western countries, or a ban on excessive interest. Thus a lax view of Islamic banking would exclude only back-street moneylenders and pawnbrokers and include modern bank lending. A distinction has also been made between interest earned on passive investments such as bonds and bank deposits, and interest earned on productive industrial loans. For all practical purposes, there is now no distinction between different forms or sources of interest. All interest, whether deemed usurious or not in Western eyes, is *Haram*.

One aspect of Islamic banking that should make Western bankers both comfortable and uncomfortable is that a Koran source distinguishes between interest and trade, and urges Muslims to receive only the principal sum loaned, that principal should only being taken back subject to the ability of the borrower to repay it. The distinction between interest and trade allows various Islamic financial instruments of a 'mark-up' character for deferred payment or early payment discounts, trade financing commissions and leasing type transactions that fit neatly into a Western bank's balance sheet. Creating liability structures is therefore relatively straightforward. However, the element of repayment 'only if able to' makes lending an uncomfortable proposition. Close attention must be paid to the meaning of 'ability to repay' and what triggers an inability to do so. Can a borrower unable to repay continue to trade?

Of course, in a suitably structured Islamic trade finance transaction title to the goods purchased by the bank B from supplier C is retained by the bank B until it is paid for by A, the end buyer of the goods and the client of the bank seeking the goods from supplier C and the financing from bank B. Such transactions may be compared with Western leases or hire-purchase agreements. And strictly speaking, the goods end-purchaser A is not obliged to buy the goods from the bank B. So B could end up with delivery of the goods from C but no end-buyer.

In Iran, which has an Islamic-only banking system, the conversion to Islamic modes has been much slower on the bank asset side than on the deposit side. Apparently only half of the resources available to the private sector are utilized and those mainly in short-term facilities such as commercial and trade transactions. In Pakistan, which has a dual system, there is also a concentration of bank assets on short-term trade credits rather than on long-term financing. The slower pace of conversion on the asset side is claimed to be the result of inadequately trained staff. To me it looks like traditional risk-aversion. Islamic loans are a good deal more risky than conventional interest-bearing, securitized loans. That, of course, is part of the point of Islamic finance. No pain – no gain. Even in such Islamic banking centres, profit and loss sharing is low (37 per cent and 13 per cent of assets in Iran and Pakistan respectively).

There is no need for me to justify the need for Islamic banking services and the prohibition of interest. It just exists through the religious beliefs of a bank's Muslim client base. One can explain away the prohibition of the eating of pork by Muslims and Jews as a result of sanitary measures thousands of years ago that were institutionalized, or the Catholic eating of fish on Fridays at a time when it represented self-sacrifice, but such practices are sincerely held and the reasons seldom questioned by the faithful. But it is worth looking at the reasons for Islamic banking put forward by some to assist with understanding and innovation.

There are various economic and rational reasons put forward as to why interest is banned in Islam. Some say that interest as a fixed cost of production is a brake on employment. There is also a view that interest causes monetary crises and exacerbates trade cycles. Other proponents say that the unearned aspect of interest makes it exploitative of labour. But then interest is only one of many ways of generating exploitative profits. Profits are *Hallal* under Islam. The fact that property rental is considered *Hallal*, but capital rental is not might seem inconsistent. The distinction is justified on the grounds that property rental has a determined benefit, whereas capital rental does not, and that property is subject to wear and tear, whilst cash under a bed is always worth the same in cash terms.

Of course, money is eroded in purchasing power terms, so should the inflation element of interest be deemed *Hallal*? Perhaps, but in practice the Islamic banking authorities have not accepted the arguments in favour of indexation. Like for like must be returned to the lender – gold for gold, barley for barley, etc. So the practical Islamic financial engineering challenge is to not lend money, but something liquid and freely exchangeable into money, but guaranteed or likely to increase in line with the interest rate forgone. Purists would phrase the challenge such: to invest in long-term development, yet at the same time manage to accommodate the liquidity requirements of both the individuals and the regulatory bodies concerned. Be this through money, goods, products or services, the purpose is to encourage economic growth, at a 'sustainable' level.

The cost of capital is recognized in Islam as a production cost, but the preferential nature of interest on profits that is not deemed acceptable. Profit and loss sharing (PLS) with the profit sharing ratio pre-determined is, however, acceptable. But how about some form of undated preference shares which are regarded by banking regulators as equity-like and tier one capital? Issuers of these shares do not have to repay the principal and can 'pass' or not pay the fixed rate dividend if there is no dividend paid on the firms' equity. Unlike under normal bond issues or bank lending, non-payment of interest does not lead to default. So one could argue that the rate of return is not fixed but variable and linked to the ability to repay if it can be zero if the borrower genuinely cannot afford to repay and automatically deferred until the borrower can repay.

I put the case for preference shares as being *Hallal* to an Islamic banking researcher. The following was his response: preference shares would be un-Islamic as both the preference and ordinary holders have equal interests in the specific company. To say then that the preference holder has a right foremost to dividends may be seen as discriminatory and unfair. Equally in the case of an exceptional profit, the preference holder is now disadvantaged with just his basic guarantee; again unfair. Can this be associated with profit sharing? Quite possibly. However profit sharing is usually between the financier and entrepreneur, not between the financier and his co-financier. Even in the case of a pre-determined ratio between two separate financiers on a specific project you do not qualify for a fixed return, rather a percentage of the return – no fixed element as would be suggested by the preference share holder.

I am not convinced by the counter argument, but I quote it to illustrate the interpretative nature of Islamic banking, the scope for creative thinking and the need for powers of persuasion.

Key Islamic financial instruments

Mudaraba

Under the principle of no pain, no gain, no-one is entitled to any addition to the principal sum if he does not share in the risks involved. The capital provider or rabbulmal may 'invest' through an entrepreneur borrower or *Mudarib*, hence the name of the structure; Profits are shared on a pre-agreed basis but losses, if any, however, are wholly suffered by the *Rabbulmal*. This financing structure is called *Mudaraba*, and to me looks like non-recourse project finance. Essentially *Mudaraba* represents a 'sleeping partnership'. According to *Sharia*, profits arising from a *Mudaraba* arrangement can be divided in any proportion between the two contracting parties as agreed upon at the time of the contract; but losses, if any, will fall on the financier only. *Mudaraba* is similar to *Shirka*.

Shirka

Shirka is a partnership between two or more persons. There are two types, *Shirka al-milk* (non-contractual) and *Shirka ul-uqud* (contractual). In the case of the contracting partnership, if the entrepreneur goes beyond the contractual limits, then he is liable for the loss.

Musharaka

Financing through equity participation is called *Musharaka*. Not being familiar with Arabic, I remember the name by likening it to share holdings. Here the partners or shareholders use their capital through a joint venture, Limited Partnership to generate a profit. Profits or losses will be split between the shareholders according to some agreed pre-formula linked but not solely linked to the investment ratio. Technically there are no fixed rules, though the use of the investment ratio is deemed fair. But again, this has to take into account the resources contributed by each party, not necessarily financial, such as experience and expertise.

Mudaraba and *Musharaka* represent the desired forms of Islamic banking even though their current use is not significant. Islamic bank depositors act as *Rabbulmals* and place funds with the bank. The bank is the *Mudarib* on its liability side with respect to the depositors. The bank uses the funds on the *Mudaraba* or *Musharaka* basis or any other Islamically approved basis with clients in search of funding. Here the bank is the *Rabbulmal* with respect to the end-users of the funds. Under such a scenario the bank acts as a principal. The bank may also act in an off-balance sheet capacity as a fee-earning agent on behalf of the fund providers and/or fund seekers or as a traditional fund manager investing in a diversified portfolio of *Musharaka* contracts.

Retail Islamic banking products

At a retail level, Islamic banks provide current, savings and investment accounts.

The current account is basically a safekeeping or *Alwadiah* account and used for day-to-day cash management. It is very similar to such accounts in conventional banks. No return is paid to depositors. The instant access accounts allow the depositors to withdraw their money on demand and permit the bank to use the depositors' money. Cheque-books are provided along with bill payment facilities, bank drafts, bills of exchange and travellers' cheques. Credit cards are unlikely to be provided, but debit cards do not seem to be a problem. Most banks have no charges for such accounts. Some banks charge to cover administration. But often such accounts are cross-subsidized by another profit-generating business in the organization for the sole purpose of marketing a no-cost account to attract Islamic deposits and gain goodwill amongst their customer base.

Alwadiah structures are also used for higher return savings accounts. Banks may as they see fit pay the savers a return, depending on their own profitability. This seems to be allowed as the bank's payment, if any, is level and is not determined in advance. Savings account holders do not have the same level of service as current account holders, but get savings books and instant or short notice access. There may or may not be a service charge incurred. Losses are not, in practice, passed on to depositors and are absorbed through the banks' reserves.

The investment accounts use the *Mudaraba* format. Deposits are fixed-term and cannot generally be cashed in before maturity. The profit-sharing ratio varies between institutions and could be a function of the bank's profitability or that of the portfolio of end-borrowers. In practice there is only profit-sharing and no loss-sharing for retail investors. The lower risk means a lower profit share. Whilst deposit terms are fixed, sometimes they may be withdrawn prior to the set date. However this incurs heavy penalties – similar to what you would expect on a fixed-rate deposit or mortgage account with a building society or bank. But it is not clear to me how these penalties square with Islamic ethics.

There are considerable variations on the *Mudaraba* principle. The Islamic Bank of Bangladesh has been offering profit and loss sharing deposit accounts, PLS special notice deposit accounts, and PLS Term Deposit accounts. Bank Islam Malaysia provides wholesale and retail investment accounts, both on the PLS principle. The frequency of payment is another variable. Profits are declared and distributed monthly in Malaysia, whilst in Egypt there is a quarterly distribution. In Bangladesh and Pakistan distributions tend to be half-yearly.

A common thread is the short-term liquid nature of the deposits. Long-term mortgage-type finance is hard to come by. The longest-term deposits appear to be raised in Malaysia. Even there almost all the deposits are under two years in maturity.

Murabaha (or Morabaha)

As I indicated earlier, the vast majority of Islamic financial transactions measured by principal does not involve a share of profit but generates a locked-in return. The *Mudaraba* and *Musharaka* transactions are often seen on the retail liability side of Islamic banks. The asset side, retail and wholesale is a good deal risky. The most common such financial instrument is the 'mark-up' structure called *Murabaha*. I liken it to the similar sounding 'repo' or sale and repurchase agreement used in the West. The only Islamic transactions that I have personally concluded have been of the *Murabaha* type.

In a *Murabaha* transaction, the bank finances the purchase of an asset by buying it on behalf of its client. The bank then adds a 'mark-up' in its sale price to its client who pays for it on a deferred basis. The 'cost-plus' nature of *Murabaha* sounds very much like the interest-into-capital-gains manipulations of tax-avoiders. Islamic banks are supposed to take a genuine commercial risk between the purchase of the asset from the seller and the sale of the asset to the person requiring the goods. The bank stands in between the buyer and the supplier and is liable if anything goes wrong. There is thus some form of guarantee with respect to the quality of the goods provided by the bank to the end-user in the strict form of *Murabaha*. Title to the goods financed may pass to the bank's client at the outset or on deferred payment. It is argued that the services provided by Islamic banks are substantially different from those of money lenders.

Many organizations use LIBOR as the reference basis for their mark-ups as being the normal market rate with a small percentage for the firm's profit. Is this Islamic? Most market participants seem to think so and LIBOR is the standard benchmark for negotiating such structures.

Baimuajjal

It is deemed acceptable to charge higher prices for deferred payments. Such transactions are regarded as trades and not loans. Property financing on such a deferred payment basis is called *Baimuajjal*.

A bank acquires a good for a client which it sells directly or through a subsidiary. It enables a buyer to finance his purchase on a deferred basis by accepting a mark-up on the market price of the commodity for payment in instalments or lump sum. The financier in this case earns a pre-determined profit without having any risk. This practice is not widely used in the industry, and some look down on it as *'financial engineering'*. Strictly the price cannot include charges for deferring payments.

Ijara

An Islamic form of leasing is called *Ijara*. Here the banks buy machinery or other equipment and lease it out under instalment plans to end-users. As in Western leasing there may be an option to buy the goods built into the contracts. The instalments consist of rental for use and part-payment. *Ijara wa iqtina* is renting, then purchasing at the end of contract.

Baisalam

When a manufacturer seeks to finance the production of goods, he seeks *Baisalam* financing. This involves the bank paying for the producer's goods at a discount before they have been delivered or even made. It is thus similar to bankers' acceptance financing in the West.

Baisalam involves the advance payment for goods to be delivered later. There is no sale unless goods exist at time of deal except where the goods are defined and a date is fixed. This sounds like commodity futures with a difference. But a central condition is the advance payment and parties cannot reserve the option of rescinding the contract. However if there is a product defect on delivery, then there is redress. *Baisalam* is typically used to fund agricultural production to help a farmer to buy seed, receiving a portion of the crops to sell at market.

'Certificates of sale'

It has been suggested that consumers buying consumables on credit would issue 'certificates of sale' similar to letters of credit. These could be encashed by the seller at the bank at a discount. This seems very similar in structure to *Baisalam*.

Prizes and bonuses

Iran and Pakistan have both attempted to fully Islamize the entire banking system. Iran converted to Islamic banking in August 1983 with a three-year transition period. In Iran, banks accept current and savings deposits without paying any return. The banks are permitted to offer bonuses and prizes on these deposits very similar to the UK's premium bonds. This is apparently not regarded as gambling by the Iranian Islamic banking units.

It is interesting to note that the UK bank Alliance & Leicester launched something similar in 1999. Everyone who opened a savings account in selected weeks in June and July 1999 was entered into a prize draw to double their money. But I am not sure if this is entirely legal. When I tried to introduce something similar for another British retail bank in 1985, I was advised that the UK's National Savings had a monopoly on such structures. So be careful of borrowing structures from elsewhere and inadvertently falling foul of your own laws and regulations. Some structures have a government monopoly or can only be issued under licence.

No fee accounts

There is a substantial Muslim population in South Africa and they are serviced by two small Islamic banks. The main product being offered is the 'no fee' current account which is also provided by the conventional banks by arrangement. Transaction charges are waived and interest is not paid on current accounts. Interest is charged on loans by conventional banks.

'Gifts'

Gifts to depositors are given entirely at the discretion of the Islamic banks on the basis of the minimum balance. These gifts may be monetary or non-monetary and are based on the banks' returns.

Other Islamic products proposed are tradable Islamic certificates of deposit, tradable certificates for investment and income sharing bonds.

Key features of Islamic banking

An analysis of the products suggests that Islamic banking has six key features:

(a) It is free of interest.
(b) It is trade-related and there is a perceived 'genuine' need for the funds.

(c) In its purest form, it is equity-related.

(d) It is meant to avoid exploitation – no usury.

(e) It invests ethically.

(f) There are retail and wholesale applications.

Interest free

The avoidance of interest has been abused by those who merely seek to be seen to be Islamic bankers. Many convert interest into capital gains and find a Koranic justification. The rules have been tightened progressively as they have been in tax avoidance.

Trade-related

I am not going to criticize devices converting interest to capital gains, as all such instruments have to show some underlying commercial need and therefore probably go some way towards the Islamic objectives. There are Western parallels with commercial paper and bankers' acceptances which also have to be trade-related. Many emerging markets, under their exchange control regimes, insist that all overseas financing or foreign exchange transactions have to be trade-related.

Equity-related

It has been suggested that 'pure Islamic banking' involves profit and loss sharing or equity participation in the *Mudaraba* and *Musharaka* forms. There is no pre-determined interest income for the lender, or in this case, the investor. The investor's return is uncertain. Sounds good and just the sort of venture capital financing many in the West have been demanding of their risk-averse banks.

I am reminded of the UK's 'Section 233 loans' developed soon after I started my banking career with Barclays Bank in 1979. Very simplistically, it was deemed by the UK tax authorities in Section 233 of the taxes act that if the borrower's payment was not fixed but linked to the current income of the firm, then the payment was not 'interest' but was 'dividend'. Dividends and interest were and are still treated differently under UK tax law. UK banks were, by and large, lenders and not equity investors. So the dividend income was useful in being used to offset dividend payments to the banks' own shareholders. Similarly there were indebted companies that were unprofitable in the UK but profitable overseas. So by converting interest to dividends they were able to offset overseas dividend income with the new UK dividends payable to UK banks. So we created a 'preference share' type of product where the dividend payable on the debt was the normal market interest rate payable by the firm, plus a minuscule percentage of the firm's profits. The rest is history. We got away with it until the Inland Revenue changed the rules. Could such a product with a nominal linking to profitability be deemed to be Islamic? Maybe.

So devices can be created so that pre-determined 'interest' can be made to look like pre-determined capital gains. Also a tiny bit of uncertainty may be introduced into the equation. But there is also a requirement to avoid exploitation. What if under a profit-sharing arrangement, because of the entrepreneur's poor bargaining position and the banker's monopoly status, the bank received 95 per cent of a venture's profits? Would this be deemed Islamic? Perhaps. There do not appear to be hard and fast rules that determine fair profit sharing ratios.

Usury – An international review

Some say that prostitution is the oldest profession; history actually suggests that the oldest profession may indeed be that of the moneylender.

MARTIN ARMSTRONG,
Princeton Economic Institute

Under the current interpretation of the rules governing Islamic banking, usury and *Riba* are regarded as synonymous. The prohibition is on interest and not just on usurious interest. In practice, there appears to be more emphasis on the prohibition and restructuring of interest than on the potentially exploitative aspect of financing.

It is worth noting there is nothing new or particularly Islamic or Christian about usury or interest controls. In the 24th century BC Manu established a rate ceiling of 24 per cent in India. Later, Hammurabi, King of Babylon, authored laws around the 19th century BC which established a cap on lending rates. On loans of grain, which were repayable in kind, the maximum rate of interest was limited to 33⅓ per cent per annum. On loans of silver, the maximum legal rate was 20 per cent, although it appears that in some cases rates of 25 per cent per annum were charged. The law remained for most of the next 12 centuries, but as with any law, 'regulatory arbitrage' took place and was subsequently eliminated. Unfair practices also existed. For example, creditors were forbidden from calling a loan made to a farmer prior to harvest. If the crop failed due to weather conditions, all interest on the loan would be cancelled for that year. In the case of houses, due to the scarcity of wood, a door could be used as collateral and was considered to be separate from a house. The sixth century Greeks, through the laws of Solon, lifted all maximum limitations on the legal rate of interest a moneylender might charge. The temple at Delphi was the 'City' or 'Wall Street' of the Greek Empire lending money for interest regularly. Credit regulation was once again part of the legal code at the start of the Roman Empire. The legal limitation on interest was established at 8⅓ per cent in the fifth century BC. Julius Caesar's attempts to control interest rates could well have been the real reason for his assassination. Many of the Roman senators at the time were the main moneylenders. *(source: A Brief History of World Credit and Interest Rates, 3000 BC to the Present, by Martin A. Armstrong, Copyright Princeton Economic Institute 1987)*

Back to the present day, quite a few Western countries have

usury laws that prohibit excessive interest rates. The UK's usury laws, which prevented 'excessive' interest, were abolished in 1854. South Africa and the US still have usury laws. Usury results when a lender charges more than the legal amount of interest permitted in that geographical area. Usury percentage limits vary by state, and at least one state, Virginia, has no usury limit. Today most of the states have had their ability to limit interest rates curtailed by overriding US Federal law. Higher than permissible rates have been regarded by US Federal banking authorities as penalty fees and insurance premiums. And the federal rate limits are high.

In some states there is no restriction on the rates used for lending to incorporated entities. The controls are often on lending to persons. The usury rate usually is variable depending on market rates. In September 1998 in North Dakota it was 10.556 per cent. California has recently imposed strict consumer-lending limits. But these only apply to state banks and not to national banks. The California Constitution allows parties to contract for interest on a loan primarily for personal, family or household purposes at a rate not exceeding 10 per cent per annum (compound annual percentage rate). The allowable rate in California is 5 per cent over the amount charged by the Federal Reserve Bank of San Francisco on advances to member banks on the 25th day of the month before the loan. The usury laws do not apply to any real-estate broker if the loan is secured by real estate. This applies whether or not he or she is acting as a real-estate broker. The limitations also do not apply to most lending institutions such as banks, credit unions, finance companies, pawnbrokers, etc. State laws place limitations on some of these loans, but at a higher percentage rate than the usury laws listed above.

Time payment contracts such as retail instalment contracts are not generally treated as loans and the usury laws normally do not apply to them. There are no limits on finance charges for the purchase of personal, family and household goods or services at this time. The maximum interest rate for car loans is almost 22 per cent. Banks also treat interest charges for third-party credit cards such as Visa, MasterCard and American Express as not being subject to usury law limitations.

In transactions for the purchase of goods or services which are not for personal, family or household purposes, there are normally no limits to finance charges except those set by the parties. Limited liability companies and limited liability partnerships can no longer assert usury as a defence in civil recovery actions. The usury interest limit that applies to limited liability companies and limited partnerships has been raised from 30 per cent per annum to 50 per cent per annum to equate to the level that applies to corporations.

But there is a problem with usury laws as I saw them in South Africa. If there is a particularly risky investment and an interest rate limit, then banks will simply not lend. The poorest will find themselves deprived of financing, and under a free market there will be a shift to quality or to those that do not really need financing. Unless there is government-imposed mandatory or tax-driven lending to certain sectors or public opinion pressure, certain sectors or individuals deemed risky by the banks will simply not get the funding required.

The emphasis on equity type transactions in Islamic banking, especially the *Mudaraba* mode, has been criticized by some for not addressing the exploitative issue.

Ethical investments

Islamic investments have to avoid undesirable sectors. In that this aspect of Islamic banking is little different from many Western 'ethical' investment funds. Ethical Financial is a UK investment adviser that arranges ethical investments for private clients. In its 1997 brochure, Ethical outlines the following ethical philosophy. Its selection process follows two paths.

(1) The selection of companies which positively contribute to the environment. Investment is made in companies that support and actively encourage the following:

- *environment protection*
- *pollution control*
- *conservation and recycling*

- *safety and security*
- *medicine and healthcare*
- *concerned, caring management*
- *equal opportunity provision for employees*
- *sanctity and dignity of human life.*

(2) Companies involved in the following activities, as far as practicable, are excluded from the Ethical Fund portfolio:

- *armaments and nuclear weapons*
- *animal exploitation and experimentation*
- *oppressive regimes*
- *alcohol and tobacco*
- *environmentally damaging practices*
- *embryonic research*
- *poor employment practices*
- *pornography*
- *gambling.*

There is a considerable overlap between Ethical's objectives and those of many of the Islamic investment funds. *Moneywise*, June 1998, had a supplement, 'A Guide to Ethical and Green Investment'. It detailed 25 green and ethical unit/investment trusts, listing 39 towards the end, and estimating there to be in excess of GBP2 billion in such funds.

Retail and wholesale applications

Islamic investments apply to wholesale and retail clients. In the West, retail Islamic investments are only offered to high net worth clients. For example Robert Fleming offer the Oasis Fund with a minimum subscription of USD50,000. There seems to be a surprising absence of products available to Islamic retail clients in the European Union. There are 1.2 million Muslims residing in the UK and even larger numbers in France (3 million) and Germany

(2.9 million). AL-Bait (The International Investor), in association with Pictet & Cie, also offer high net worth Islamic products. Arab Bank offers an investment account, but again with minimum subscription of USD10,000. The Hallal Mutual Investment Fund, however, has set up a unit trust with a minimum of GBP250. But it is far from a household name. Amongst major European banks, I am only aware of Barclays Private Bank that offers Islamic accounts, but then only to its high net worth clients.

Islamic Investment Banking Unit at the United Bank of Kuwait in London offers *Hallal* mortgages. But so far market penetration has been limited.

Islamic derivatives

It is generally assumed that the term 'Islamic derivatives' is a contradiction. The requirements of derivatives and rules of Shariah at first sight are diametrically opposed and all derivatives are therefore *Haram*. But it is important to recall the generalized definition I use of a financial derivative. It is simply a financial instrument that is derived from another financial instrument or a combination of such instruments. It is argued that as derivatives 'unquestionably' involve interest or interest-based products they are contaminated and should be prohibited. Well, derivatives only involve interest if one or both parties using the derivative seeks to hedge the derivative. It could be argued that *Murabaha* could involve interest if the parties seek to match the interest-free but guaranteed return product with an interest-bearing equivalent. Islamic banking derivatives should be perfectly acceptable so long as they do not involve interest.

In Malaysia there is a dual financial system. An Islamic banking system works alongside a conventional interest-bearing banking system. But there is only one purely Islamic bank compared with 26 dual-system banks offering Islamic windows. These dual-system banks do not completely separate the Islamic banking units from the rest of the bank, and there is inevitably a crossover of the effects of derivatives from the conventional system into the Islamic system.

Most of the research into the acceptability of Islamic derivatives has been accordingly carried out in Malaysia. There have also been developments in Bahrain.

I would argue that *Baisalam*, which involves the pre-payment for goods, is indeed an Islamic banking derivative and can be regarded as a kind of forward contract. I would argue that it boils down to intentions. Alcohol is prohibited under Islam. But alcohol is used as a disinfectant in surgery. Alcohol is also used as anti-freeze in cars. Wheat futures can be used as a gambling tool. But wheat or oil futures as used by farmers or oil producer can help them manage their businesses and iron out economic cycles. Gold and silver are generally deemed to be money substitutes and there-fore dealings in them are regarded as *Haram*. Options are but insurance policies. Just as *Takaful* is an acceptable Islamic form of insurance, options for delivery of commodities by a producer of such a commodity should be acceptable. So also should options or forward contracts on any of the Islamic financial instruments men-tioned.

The acid test seems to be the presence or otherwise of an underlying trade transaction to justify the derivative transaction. There will undoubtedly be developments that attempt to make Islamic derivative contracts look and feel like non-derivative con-tracts. The process is similar to that in the early days of derivatives. There was a problem with the tax treatment of FRAs. So we cre-ated a synthetic FRA to overcome the problem. Such a product could be tweaked to serve as an Islamic derivative.

Just as it took decades for conventional banking regulators, tax authorities and auditors to catch up with developments in financial derivatives, it will be a long time before Islamic deriva-tives are deemed to be acceptable. The developments will prove to be very similar to the developments in derivatives in the late 1970s. The Islamic banking derivatives winners will be those who remember or research into financial history rather than the rocket scientists.

Conclusion

Whilst Islamic bankers have sought to avoid excessive risk through *Murabaha*, *Ijara* and *Baisalam*, the essential element of most such deals is the linking to a genuine identifiable trade transaction. Islamic finance seekers thus have to open themselves up to their banks even more than their Western counterparts and can only obtain finance for genuine needs. *Musharaka* and *Mudaraba* are more difficult to obtain. Firms or individuals cannot borrow to repay another bank. General-purpose finance or borrowing for consumption purposes, overdrafts and swing lines do not exist. Nevertheless, Islamic banks are more risky than their Western counterparts through their riskier equity and trade financing businesses. Credit risk management skills with the comfort of collateral are just not good enough. Project evaluation and equity valuation skills are essential.

Higher than normal reserves are required, diversification of assets is needed to protect against losses, and diversification of liabilities is required for liquidity management.

There is the issue of money creation and the multiplier effect through the use of *Mudaraba*. Some strict proponents of Islamic banking advocate the imposition of 100 per cent reserve requirements.

Such 'Islamic' business is not unknown in Western banking. It is called investment banking and requires sound asset and liability management. There are counterparts of Western banking in almost all forms of Islamic banking. There are Islamic versions of repos, leasing, unit trusts, hire purchase, equity investments, venture capital and non-recourse project finance.

There are also non-Islamic parallels with ethical investment fund management. Geoff Pearson, the manager of the J. Sainsbury pension fund, recently said that 'the pensions minister was right to ask trustees to disclose their policy on ethical and social issues' (*Financial Times*, 20 September 1998), and Nottinghamshire County Council is set to allocate 15 per cent of its pension fund to ethical investments (*Financial Times*, 15 September 1998). The

UK's Co-operative Bank a few years ago proudly advertised its recall of loans to 'undesirable' armaments, animal-testing, tobacco and alcohol companies. It appears that only one of its clients was in such businesses, but the favourable publicity it received led to a considerable increase in its accounts from 'green' clients. Green also just happens to be the Islamic colour. Islamic banks are also supposed to make charitable contributions. In the West, there are a number of affinity credit cards which make small contributions to the client's chosen charity. Perhaps, cynically, BCCI sought to display green credentials amongst its clients by having its credit card linked to an environmental charity.

This is neither an economics nor a social studies textbook. It is nevertheless useful to examine the rationale of Islamic banking so as to understand the product development process. The theoretical basic principle of Islamic banking is to encourage growth and not to make an 'unreasonable' profit. Subsequently any effort between an entrepreneur and a financier has to be on an equal footing to further the cause of mutual growth, reducing the gap between the rich and the poor – in theory if not necessarily in practice. It could be compared with the idea of various 'stakeholders' in an economy.

I must stress that this appendix has not attempted to be a clear treatise on the rules and regulations of Islamic banking. It should, however, help a non-Islamic bank to satisfy actual or potential customer demand or a non-Islamic organization to accept Islamic funding.

Glossary

Alwadiah = safe-keeping

Baimuajjal = deferred-payment sale

Baisalam = pre-paid purchase

Baitulmal = treasury

Hallal = lawful

Haram = unlawful

Ijara = leasing

Mudaraba = profit-sharing

Mudarib = entrepreneur-borrower

Muqarada = *Mudaraba*

Murabaha = cost-plus or mark-up

Musharaka = equity participation

Qard Hasan = benevolent loan (interest free)

Qirad = *Mudaraba*

Rabbulmal = owner of capital

Riba = interest

Shariah = Islamic law

Shirka = *Musharaka*

Appendix 5: Bibliography

There is, of course, a huge literature on the topic of financial instruments and innovation. There follows here but a sample of books on the subject that I have found entertaining, informative or both. They may provide a useful alternative view.

Braddock	(1997)	*Derivatives Demystified.*	Wiley
Brealey	(1991)	*Principles of Corporate Finance.* 4th edition	McGraw Hill
Dawkins	(1996)	*River Out of Eden: A Darwinian View of Life.*	Basic Books
Dufey & Giddy	(1994)	*The International Money Market.* 2nd edition	Prentice Hall
Fabozzi	(1995)	*The Handbook of Fixed Income Securities.* 4th edition	Irwin Professional Publishing
Follett	(1993)	*A Dangerous Fortune.*	Delacorte Press
Francis	(1994)	*The Handbook of Interest Rate Risk Management.*	Irwin Professional Publishing
Galitz	(1995)	*Financial Engineering.* revised edition	FT Pitman Publishing
Giddy	(1995)	*Global Financial Markets.*	Heath
Gleick	(1998)	*Chaos.*	Vintage
Holliwell	(1997)	*The Financial Risk Manual.*	FT Pitman Publishing
Hull	(1995)	*Introduction to Futures and Options Markets.* 2nd edition	Prentice Hall
Hull	(1997)	*Options, Futures and Other Derivatives Securities.* 3rd edition	Prentice Hall
Jett	(1999)	*Black and White on Wall Street.*	William Morrow
Kendall	(1997)	*Risk Management for Executives.*	FT Pitman Publishing

Konishi, Dattatreya	(1996)	*The Handbook of Derivative Instruments*. 2nd edition	Irwin Professional Publishing
Lederman, Park	(1994)	*The Global Bond Markets*.	Heinemann Asia
Leeson	(1996)	*Rogue Trader*.	Little, Brown & Co.
Levine	(1999)	*Derivatives: Law & Documentation*.	Sweet & Maxwell
Lewis	(1989)	*Liar's Poker*.	Hodder & Stoughton
Masson	(1995)	*The Treasurer's Handbook*.	Probus
Mattoo	(1997)	*Structured Derivatives*.	FT Pitman Publishing
Miller	(1997)	*Merton Miller on Derivatives*.	Wiley
Park, Schoenfeld	(1994)	*Pacific Rim Futures & Options Markets*.	Heinemann Asia
Patel	(1997)	*The Mind of a Trader*.	FT Pitman Publishing
Ravindran	(1998)	*Customised Derivatives*.	McGraw Hill
Redhead	(1994)	*Introduction to Financial Investment*.	Prentice Hall
Saunders	(1994)	*Financial Institutions Management*.	Irwin Professional Publishing
Scott-Quinn & Walmsley	(1998)	*The Impact of Credit Derivatives on Securities Markets*.	ISMA
Smith, Smithson	(1990)	*The Handbook of Financial Engineering*.	Harper & Row
Stigum	(1990)	*The Money Markets*.	Irwin Professional Publishing
Taylor	(1996)	*Mastering Derivatives Markets*.	FT Pitman Publishing
The Globecon Group	(1995)	*Derivatives Engineering*.	Irwin Professional Publishing
Walmsley	(1992)	*The Foreign Exchange and Money Markets Guide*.	Wiley
Walmsley	(1996)	*International Money and Foreign Exchange Markets: An Introduction*	Wiley

Author's publications

(1978) 'Inflation and the term structure of interest rates: The UK Experience', *Pioneering Economics*, CEDAM Padua, Italy.

(1990) 'Break forwards: a synthetic option hedging instrument', in *The Handbook of Financial Engineering*, Wiley, New York.

'Perpetual swaps: managing currency translation exposures', *The Treasurer*, London, November 1991.

'Why Delphi has the answers; Delphi duration, an A/LM technique', *Balance Sheet Magazine*, London, April 1992.

'To hedge or not to hedge? Directors liable for losses', *IFR swaps*, London, 28 April 1993.

'Hedging Yardsticks', *Treasury Management International*, London, July/August 1993.

'To hedge or not to hedge? Esta es la cuestión', *Cinco Días*, Madrid, 16 July 1993.

'Hedge choice & performance measurement', Cover article, *ACTSA Newsletter* (Assn Corp. Treasurers, Southern Africa), Johannesburg, August 1993.

'Los Derivados, sin mitos (1)' *Cinco Días*, Madrid, 5 October 1993.

'Los Derivados, sin mitos (2)' *Cinco Días*, Madrid, 6 October 1993.

'¿Derivados al por menor?' *Cinco Días*, Madrid, 22 March 1994.

'APRs – misleading, misused or just plain misunderstood', *The Times*, London, 8 April 1995.

'For your benefit: An analysis of benefit functions in treasury and portfolio management', *IFR Financial Products*, London, April 1995.

'Competitive pricing of islamic financial products', *Horizon*, Institute of Islamic Banking & Insurance, London, May 1995.

'Demystifying derivatives', *Treasury Today*, Institute of Chartered Accountants in England & Wales, London, June 1995.

'Liberalisation of financial markets in Korea', *AmCham Journal*, American Chamber of Commerce in Korea, July/August 1996.

'Korean financial markets: Two steps forward – one step backward', *Korea Times*, 19 August 1996.

'Corea – mercados financieros', *Cinco Días*, Madrid, 16 October 1996.

'Derivatiphobia', *The Bridge Guide to Corporate Treasury in Asia 1997*, Hong Kong, March 1997.

'Creative Thinking', *The Pagoda Pivot*, Rotary Club of Seoul, Korea, 16 April 1997.

'Regulatory change required to meet blurred financial edges', *Financial Times*, London, 23 July 1997.

'Study history for a lesson on liquidity', *Financial Times*, London, 5 December 1997.

'Burgernomics or Economistics', *The Economist*, London, 6 December 1997.

'Credit derivatives folly', *Sunday Business*, London, 18 March 1998.

'Demystifying Derivatives: A cure for Derivatiphobia', *Forex and Global Markets*, London, Summer 1998.

'Virtually no travelling', *Financial Times*, London, 25 September 1998.

'Creative thinking: How to capture the big new IDEA', *Global Trading*, London, 3rd Quarter 1998.

'Derivatiphobia: a director's guide to derivatives', *Treasury Management International*, London, December 1998.

'Survey on the use by professionals of electronic commerce', Delphi Communication, March 1999.

'Islamic Banking', *Princeton Economics Journal*, Princeton Economics Intl., Princeton, USA, 1st Quarter 1999.

'Less Technophilia – have faith in fools', Leader Column, Treasury Management International, London, April 1999.

'Halo effect of the @', *Financial Times*, London, 3 May 1999.

'Bid bye bye to the fortuity of cricket's toss', *Financial Times*, London, 3 May 1999.

'My winning formula for grand prix racing', *Financial Times*, London, 19 June 1999.

'How to capture the big IDEA', *Treasury Management International*, London, July/August 1999.

Website: www.dc3.co.uk/publish.htm

Index